New Directions for
Adult and Continuing
Education

Susan Imel
Jovita M. Ross-Gordon
COEDITORS-IN-CHIEF

S0-BZP-115

Adult Education in the Rural Context: People, Place, and Change

Jeffrey A. Ritchey

EDITOR

Property of Library
Cape Fear Community College
Wilmington, NC

Number 117 • Spring 2008
Jossey-Bass
San Francisco

ADULT EDUCATION IN THE RURAL CONTEXT: PEOPLE, PLACE, AND CHANGE
Jeffrey A. Ritchey (ed.)
New Directions for Adult and Continuing Education, no. 117
Susan Imel, Jovita M. Ross-Gordon, Coeditors-in-Chief

© 2008 Wiley Periodicals, Inc., A Wiley Company. All rights reserved. No part of this publication may be reproduced, stored in a retrieval system, or transmitted in any form or by any means, electronic, mechanical, photocopying, recording, scanning, or otherwise, except as permitted under Section 107 or 108 of the 1976 United States Copyright Act, without either the prior written permission of the Publisher or authorization through payment of the appropriate per-copy fee to the Copyright Clearance Center, 222 Rosewood Drive, Danvers, MA 01923, (978) 750-8400, fax (978) 646-8600. The copyright notice appearing at the bottom of the first page of an article in this journal indicates the copyright holder's consent that copies may be made for personal or internal use, or for personal or internal use of specific clients, on the condition that the copier pay for copying beyond that permitted by law. This consent does not extend to other kinds of copying, such as copying for distribution, for advertising or promotional purposes, for creating collective works, or for resale. Such permission requests and other permission inquiries should be addressed to the Permissions Department, c/o John Wiley & Sons, Inc., 111 River Street, Hoboken, NJ 07030; (201) 748-6011, fax (201) 748-6008, www. wiley.com/go/permissions.

Microfilm copies of issues and articles are available in 16mm and 35mm, as well as microfiche in 105mm, through University Microfilms Inc., 300 North Zeeb Road, Ann Arbor, Michigan 48106-1346.

NEW DIRECTIONS FOR ADULT AND CONTINUING EDUCATION (ISSN 1052-2891, electronic ISSN 1536-0717) is part of The Jossey-Bass Higher and Adult Education Series and is published quarterly by Wiley Subscription Services, Inc., A Wiley Company, at Jossey-Bass, 989 Market Street, San Francisco, California 94103-1741. Periodicals Postage Paid at San Francisco, California, and at additional mailing offices. POSTMASTER: Send address changes to New Directions for Adult and Continuing Education, Jossey-Bass, 989 Market Street, San Francisco, California 94103-1741.

New Directions for Adult and Continuing Education is indexed in CIJE: Current Index to Journals in Education (ERIC); Contents Pages in Education (T&F); ERIC Database (Education Resources Information Center; Higher Education Abstracts (Claremont Graduate University); and Sociological Abstracts (CSA/CIG).

SUBSCRIPTIONS cost $85.00 for individuals and $209.00 for institutions, agencies, and libraries.

EDITORIAL CORRESPONDENCE should be sent to the Coeditors-in-Chief, Susan Imel, ERIC/ACVE, 1900 Kenny Road, Columbus, Ohio 43210-1090, e-mail: imel.l@osu.edu; or Jovita M. Ross-Gordon, Southwest Texas State University, EAPS Dept., 601 University Drive, San Marcos, TX 78666.

Cover photograph by Jack Hollingsworth@Photodisc

www.josseybass.com

CONTENTS

EDITOR'S NOTES

Except for a brief period after completing my undergraduate degree, I have lived and worked my entire life in the rural United States. As a result, I have been intrigued and somewhat troubled by the lack of interest adult educators have shown in *my* communities and *my* neighbors.

Although there has recently been a relative abundance of material produced on adult education in rural areas outside the United States (Golding, 2005/2006; Minnis, 2006; Pieck, 2005; Prins, 2006), little work has been done that focuses on the changing nature of rural adult learning and instruction in the United States. Such neglect, however, does not suggest that rural issues and rural places lack relevance in contemporary U.S. society. And it has been a pleasure to find that others around the country share this sentiment and have joined in producing this work—what I hope will be the beginning of a more sustained, wide-ranging, and long-overdue analysis of rural places by adult education researchers and practitioners alike.

This volume seeks to expand our concept of the rural United States as it explores the role that adult educators might play in this complex context. Indeed, complexity is the hallmark of this volume. Although rural areas are still composed of large expanses of open space, they nevertheless are being hit by a continuing process of suburbanization, resulting in demographic, economic, and cultural changes that challenge those teaching and learning in rural places. The chapters in this volume broadly reflect traditional ways of categorizing adult and continuing education efforts (adult basic education and literacy, English as a Second Language, workplace learning, and so forth), including work addressing the impact of technology on rural places, and some focus on that quintessentially rural adult education enterprise, the Cooperative Extension Service.

I begin this volume with a brief overview of the term *rural* and a summary of issues critical to adult and continuing educators who are working with rural populations. I examine shifts in demographics, economics, land use, and the means by which rural people engage one another and their nonrural neighbors.

In Chapter Two, Jeff Zacharakis explores the relationship between popular education and the grassroots community-based educational principles of the Cooperative Extension Service. Focusing on the relationship between community economic development and popular education, he contends that while it may seem strange to conceive of the Extension's institutionalized work as "popular," the organization's community-based, participatory mission firmly grounds it in this progressive movement.

NEW DIRECTIONS FOR ADULT AND CONTINUING EDUCATION, no. 117, Spring 2008 © 2008 Wiley Periodicals, Inc.
Published online in Wiley InterScience (www.interscience.wiley.com) • DOI: 10.1002/ace.280

In Chapter Three, Mary F. Ziegler and Dent C. Davis introduce Restin County, a remote, southern Appalachian region where residents have successfully linked basic education to community and economic development. This chapter speaks to the highly contextual nature of rural adult basic education and the potential power of strengthening partnerships across traditional boundaries.

Chapter Four addresses the challenges faced by rural English as a Second Language educators, particularly those working among migrant populations. Focusing on their experiences with the University of Michigan's Migrant Outreach Program, John McLaughlin, Maria Rodriguez, and Carolyn Madden point out the challenges that both students and teachers working with migrant communities face. Just as important, they point out the transformative potential of this work for individual participants and the communities in which they live and work.

With a series of case studies, Vivian W. Mott uses Chapter Five to address strategies for working with older adults in an increasingly complex rural environment. These cases powerfully point out that the contextual realities of rural, older adults and the subsequent rationales for their participation in continued learning vary widely from community to community and individual to individual.

As I have noted, the complexity of rural society pervades this volume. Andrew Page and Melissa Hill continue this theme in Chapter Six as they examine the diffusion of educational technologies to rural Alaskan educators. Although the discussion of rural places and technology is often reduced to the issue of access (particularly to broadband Internet), the authors point out a more complex framework for understanding the rural digital divide that also includes issues of context, capability, and content.

In Chapter Seven, Robert F. Reardon and Ann K. Brooks examine five rural workplace segments—health care, law enforcement, agriculture, education, and small business—and find that each has unique needs and barriers to learning. Rural workplaces offer specific challenges for adult educators, not the least of which is employers' willingness to see training and employee continuing education as important to organizational productivity and stability.

In Chapter Eight, Susan J. Bracken moves the discussion back out into the community, turning to the education of rural adults in nonformal settings. This work continues to interrogate our conceptions of rural places—challenging us to achieve deeper understandings of how rural residents conceive of their own educational and communal participation and to think creatively about our own research and practice in these spaces.

In the final chapter, I provide an overview of the volume and further exploration of the potential directions for continued research and study in rural adult education. Such work is surely grounded in a sensitivity for and commitment to the unique aspects of rural life. The exploration of small, closely knit communities with strong intergenerational ties and well-established social networks takes time both to access and to understand. As one of many rural residents, I hope this volume will encourage others to study rural people and rural places.

Jeffrey A. Ritchey
Editor

References

Golding, B. G. "Listening to Men Learn." *International Journal of Learning*, 2005/2006, *12*(9), 265–272.

Minnis, J. R. "Nonformal Education and Informal Economies in Sub-Saharan Africa: Finding the Right Match." *Adult Education Quarterly*, 2006, *56*(2), 119–133.

Pieck, E. "Work-Related Adult Education: Challenges and Possibilities in Poverty Areas." *International Journal of Lifelong Education*, 2005, 24(5), 419–429.

Prins, E. "Relieving Isolation, Avoiding Vices: The Social Purposes of Participation in a Salvadoran Literacy Program." *Adult Education Quarterly*, 2006, 57(1), 5–25.

JEFFREY A. RITCHEY is an assistant professor of adult and community education at Indiana University of Pennsylvania.

1

This chapter provides a brief overview of the term rural *and a summary of critical issues important to adult and continuing educators working with rural populations.*

Rural Adult Education: Current Status

Jeffrey A. Ritchey

Context. The word pervades the literature on adult and continuing education. For adult education practitioners and researchers alike, understanding the beliefs and actions of their educational place continues to be of significant concern, and rightfully so. That adults wish to have their histories, experiences, and abilities appreciated and validated has become a basic tenet of our discipline, and a thorough analysis of the educational context appears to be the only way to make this appreciation and validation possible.

In very broad terms, one aspect of context—the distribution of people in geographical space—has been broadly divided into two categories based primarily on population density. These classifications, urban and rural, have provided a convenient, if often debated, means for directing resources and categorizing populations for study and outreach. (Another common classification, suburban, has largely been subsumed within the recently developed classification of urban cluster discussed below.)

Defining Rurality

In an attempt to create a more precise picture of U.S. population distribution, various state and federal agencies have refined their definitions of *urban* and *rural*. For the casual reader, however, these sometimes conflicting descriptions do little to simplify context-related discussions. The U.S. Census Bureau distinguishes rural and urban areas by population density regardless of municipal boundaries. In the words of the Economic Research Service, the Census Bureau assesses population distributions "as they might appear from the air" (U.S. Department of Agriculture, 2007, p. 1). Urban

NEW DIRECTIONS FOR ADULT AND CONTINUING EDUCATION, no. 117, Spring 2008 © 2008 Wiley Periodicals, Inc.
Published online in Wiley InterScience (www.interscience.wiley.com) • DOI: 10.1002/ace.281

5

settlements are classified as either urbanized areas (having "an urban nucleus of 50,000 or more people" [p. 1]) or urban clusters (populations of at least twenty-five hundred but fewer than fifty thousand people). For the Census Bureau, *rural* is thus everything that is not an urbanized area or urban cluster. By this reasoning, the U.S. rural population in 2000 stood at 59.1 million, or 21 percent of the total U.S. population.

Often researchers prefer the terms *metropolitan* and *nonmetropolitan* when discussing geographical spaces (this is particularly so for the Economic Research Service). These designations, established by the U.S. Office of Management and Budget (OMB), base their designations on county data. A metropolitan area is either a central county "with one or more urbanized area" of fifty thousand or more residents or an outlying county that is "economically tied to the core counties as measured by work commuting" (U.S. Department of Agriculture, 2007, p. 1). These outlying counties are assessed as metropolitan if 25 percent of their workers commute to the central counties or if 25 percent of their industries are staffed by people commuting from central counties (reverse commuting). Simply put, outlying counties must have a significant economic tie to their central metropolitan neighbors.

Nonmetropolitan counties are all those without metropolitan ties. These nonmetropolitan areas have recently been divided into two additional categories: micropolitan (containing an urban cluster of ten thousand or more persons) and noncore or "other" counties. Using OMB definitions, there were 49.2 million nonmetropolitan U.S. residents in 2000.

It is important, however, that Census Bureau definitions of *urban* and *rural* not be confused with OMB definitions of *metropolitan* and *nonmetropolitan*. Indeed, only 59 percent of nonmetropolitan residents lived in rural areas, and a slight majority of rural residents now live in counties classified as metropolitan. It is about as clear as mud.

Nevertheless, what we call something has significance not only in tangible ways (like eligibility for funding sources) but also in more ephemeral but equally important and powerful ways. I, for example, consider myself to be from a rural community: a Pennsylvania mill town of some twenty-five hundred residents whose primary occupations revolved (when I was a child) around manufacturing (paper production), extractive industries (mining and logging), and agriculture (dairy and crop farming). My colleagues and friends today from more populous places like Pittsburgh, Harrisburg, or Philadelphia agree with my assessment, as do my current neighbors in a slightly larger community of seven thousand residents (none of whom consider themselves rural in any way). Yet according to the OMB, I was and remain a metropolitan person.

All of this is to say that concepts such as rural and urban are perhaps best defined in an emergent fashion—their meanings precipitating from the myriad stories and images weaving throughout a specific place and time (Ritchey, 2002). Indeed, it has been a long-standing criticism of statistical definition that it does not allow the contextual considerations—cultural,

New Directions for Adult and Continuing Education • DOI: 10.1002/ace

historical, political, economic, and spiritual—that appear so closely linked to concepts such as rural as well as to the effective practice of adult and continuing educators regardless of context.

The search for a more contextual definition for *rurality* is nothing new. Some twenty-five years ago, Bunce (1982) noted four categories of criteria that could be used to distinguish rural communities from their urban counterparts: demographic, political, economic, and sociocultural. More recently, discussions have centered on "rural values," or what has come to be called "rural character" and to its preservation. These conceptions also appear to be best defined at the local level, with descriptors often including "tree-lined streets, farmlands, woodlands, clean air and water, undeveloped open space, natural streambanks, natural lake shorelines, outdoor recreation opportunities and small villages and communities" (Van Buren County Community Center, 2003, p. 1).

Some scholars argue that technology and improved transportation have effectively rendered the notion of rural society obsolete (Friedland, 1982; Gallaher and Padfield, 1980; Vidich, 1980; Whatmore, 1993). Consumptive culture is as evident in small towns as in large cities, with Internet shopping, YouTube, and iTunes bringing once hard-to-obtain music, images, and merchandise to the door of even the most physically isolated consumers.

Nevertheless, most definitions of rurality center on a few key physical, social, and economic criteria (Ritchey, 2002): low population density, considerable traveling distance to market areas for either work or everyday living activities (medical doctors, restaurants, grocery stores, and so forth), limited political power, few public services, a history grounded in agriculture or extractive industries such as mining or timbering, and a high degree of cultural homogeneity. This homogeneity, however, disappears beyond the local level, as comparisons between rural towns show more diversity than do comparisons between urban areas.

All this points to the complexity of working in rural settings, where the meanings of terms such as *poverty, work, opportunity, values, education, learning, skills, family,* and *community* may be very context specific. Understanding this specificity and incorporating the articulation of meanings into educational offerings (and subsequent reflection on definitions' power to shape relationships and expectations) seems paramount.

Adult Education in Rural America

Historically, adult education has close ties to rural people and places. From union organizing to correspondence schools, from the extension service to Highlander Center, adults in remote and isolated places have engaged in formal and nonformal (and very clearly informal) learning since the nation's birth.

And there continues to be no general lack of interest in things rural. "A simple search of the Internet reveals a vast array of university research papers, government publications and special interest group analyses that address an equally daunting list of issues" about rural America (Ritchey, 2006, p. 1). Yet the literature on adult education—the journals and texts we peruse as the canon of our discipline—has paid relatively little attention to the issues important to rural places and the educative needs of rural residents. Recently I (Ritchey, 2006) completed a review of the literature addressing rural adult education in Pennsylvania. The findings of this work resonate strongly with the issues identified in national publications as both shaping and being shaped by the rural context. In turn, these issues will continue to have a powerful impact on the work of adult and continuing educators in rural communities.

Demographic Shifts. The population dynamics of the rural United States are shifting in several ways, and while "non-metropolitan populations continue to be older than metropolitan populations" (Jones, Kandel, and Parker, 2007, p. 1), this continuation is the result of both a continued loss of younger residents and an influx of retirees moving to nonmetropolitan counties. In addition, nonmetropolitan areas have seen an increase in racial and ethnic diversity. "Although non-Hispanic Whites make up 82 percent of the nonmetro population, diversity is increasing more rapidly than in previous decades" (p. 5). In particular, rural areas have seen marked increases in Hispanic and Asian residents, many of whom are younger and traditionally have larger families than do their non-Hispanic white neighbors. "The different age distributions between these two groups imply diverging social service needs and societal contributions. More elderly non-Hispanic Whites will need retirement communities, nursing homes, and home care, while young minority families will need schools, jobs, child care, and health services suited for children and young adults" (p. 7). Jensen (2006) notes that "the impact of immigration can, and often is, more acutely felt in rural communities than big cities, even if the absolute number of new comers may be much smaller" (p. 7). This impact clearly includes the changing educational needs of new rural residents.

Economic Shifts. Flora, Flora, and Fey ask, "Which is the real rural America: ski slopes of California, mines of West Virginia, farms of Iowa, or exurban resort and manufacturing communities in Georgia?" (2003, p. 3). Such images bring home the reality that rural places are more diverse one to another than are their urban counterparts. And while the image of rural America remains grounded in farming and agriculture, the economies of rural places have steadily become more reliant on industries of the new economy: health care, social and business services, and retail sales. Perhaps this has been nowhere more evident than in the impact of big box stores such as Wal-Mart in "reshaping the character of the communities" in which they reside (Institute for Rural Journalism and Community Issues, 2005, p. 2). Stone (1997) notes "strong evidence that rural communities in the United States have been more adversely impacted by the discount mass merchandisers (sometimes referred to as the Wal-Mart phenomenon) than by any other factor in recent times. Studies in Iowa have shown that some small towns lose up to 47 percent of their retail trade after 10 years of Wal-Mart stores nearby" (p. 189).

In turn, the economic reshaping of rural America predicts a corresponding educational reshaping of the rural landscape, with adult and continuing education helping to meet the ongoing training needs of new sectors while playing a critical role in reshaping traditional rural industries such as farming, mining, and logging.

Environmental and Land Use Shifts. Yet even as the economy continues its move to the service sector, rural places remain intimately linked to the land. Indeed, according to the U.S. Census Bureau, some 95 percent of the nation is rural open space (O'Toole, 2003). As a result and regardless of ownership, the stewardship of such vast tracks of natural resources is of global concern. Crop and livestock farming and commercial forestry operation have often been cited as the sources of environmental pollution, including nonpoint source water contamination and high-level emissions of greenhouse gases (Jackson-Smith, 2003). As small family farms have been replaced by corporate operations, such charges have continued.

Loss of farmland and the expansion of rural residential development also continue to be concerns. "A new housing development containing many children can provide a windfall of municipal tax revenue, as well as the peripheral jobs that help create and support rural communities including contractors, teachers, and daycare workers" (Ritchey, 2006, p. 8). Yet this development has a long-term cost. A recent study on land use in eleven rural Pennsylvania townships indicates that "residential land on average contributed less to the local municipality and school district than it required back in expenditures" and "commercial, industrial, and farm- and open land provided more than they required back in expenditures" (Kelsey, 1997, p. 2). Furthermore, MacTavish and Salamon (2003) note that rural communities experiencing residential growth have also seen significant population segregation, as new homes are constructed and existing communities isolated and overlooked. In these regions, upscale developments are constructed to attract wealthy newcomers, who bring with them their suburban expectations and sensibilities. These developments are generally constructed at the peripheries of small, rural enclaves, which then contain "poor families in what are emerging as rural slums" (MacTavish and Salamon, 2003, p. 78).

This growing disconnect between humanity and the natural world can be seen daily in my own community as commuters speed from more urbanized centers to the growing array of rural residential developments—spaces populated by people who, while living in the country, evidence little connection to or interest in their surroundings. Adult and continuing educators can play a powerful and important role in reconnecting people to this vast, natural, rural world.

New Directions for Adult and Continuing Education • DOI: 10.1002/ace

Communications Shifts. Technological innovations have transformed how information is disseminated and consumed. These innovations have long been heralded as a major means for revitalizing rural communities while maintaining their distinctive character. Research sponsored by the Pew Charitable Trust's Internet and American Life Project indicates that while 52 percent of rural Americans were using the Internet in 2003, they lag urban and suburban residents by 15 and 14 percent, respectively (Bell, Reddy, and Rainie, 2004). Furthermore, this shortfall appears directly related to other demographic and economic shifts noted in this chapter—specifically an aging population and persistent poverty. While rural residents appear ready and willing to use online communication options, research indicates this willingness is often impeded by limited Internet service provider options.

In discussing one aspect of this communications shift, e-learning, Carr-Chellman points out that often, technology "tends to disconnect people rather than connect them" (2005, p. 150). Many rural residents have seen the isolating effects of technology in their own communities and are understandably suspicious of its long-term effects on how people interact and spend their nonworking time. Adult educators will play an important function in negotiating technological shifts among rural "digital immigrants" (Prensky, 2001, p. 1) and "digital natives" alike.

Conclusion

Contrary to popular perception, the context of rural America is one of great complexity and pervasive, long-term change. For adult educators, working in such an environment demands that they take the time to better understand the changing landscape of their communities and participate in the debates that both mold and are molded by rural people and places. Such an understanding is necessary to bring all voices into the rural community discussion and help negotiate something richer and more sustainable.

For my own state of Pennsylvania, such a process is about not assimilation but negotiation (Ritchey, 2006). Expanding the discussion to the national level has not changed my belief that rural educators will be only as effective as they are willing to become participants in the creation of their respective communities. "From ESL educators to extension agents, from religious educators to e-learning providers, the process will involve both content and contextual knowledge that is blended to encourage not assimilation or enculturation but rather the creation of something new, vibrant and focused on possibility not loss" (Ritchey, 2006, p. 13). It speaks to a reexamination of what Brookfield (1995) called our "paradigmatic assumptions" (para. 6), in this case concerning what adult education is and can be in those places and with those people we have come to call *rural*.

References

Bell, P., Reddy, P., and Rainie, L. *Rural Areas and the Internet.* Pew Charitable Trust Internet and American Life Project. 2004. Retrieved May 22, 2007, from http://www.pewinternet. org/pdfs/PIP_Rural_Report.pdf.

Brookfield, S. "The Getting of Wisdom: What Critically Reflective Teaching Is and Why It Is Important." In S. D. Brookfield (ed.), *Becoming a Critically Reflective Teacher.* San Francisco: Jossey-Bass, 1995. Retrieved May 22, 2007, from http://www3.nl.edu/academics/cas/ace/facultypapers/StephenBrookfield_Wisdom.cfm.

Bunce, M. *Rural Settlement in an Urban World.* New York: St. Martin's Press, 1982.

Carr-Chellman, A. A. "The New Frontier: Web-Based Education in U.S. Culture." In A. A. Chellman (ed.), *Global Perspectives on E-Learning: Rhetoric and Reality.* Thousand Oaks, Calif.: Sage, 2005.

Flora, C. B., Flora, J. F., and Fey, S. *Rural Communities: Legacy and Change.* (2nd ed.) Boulder, Colo.: Westview Press, 2003.

Friedland, W. H. "The End of Rural Society and the Future of Rural Sociology." *Rural Sociology,* 1982, *47,* 589–608.

Gallaher, A., and Padfield, H. (eds.). *The Dying Community.* Albuquerque: University of New Mexico Press, 1980.

Institute for Rural Journalism and Community Issues. "Issues in the Rural Economy." 2005. Retrieved May 21, 2007, from http://www.uky.edu/CommInfoStudies/IRJCI/knightdrabenstott.htm.

Jackson-Smith, D. B. "The Challenges of Land Use in the Twenty-First Century." In D. L. Brown and L. E. Swanson (eds.), *Challenges for Rural America in the Twenty-First Century.* University Park: Pennsylvania State University Press, 2003.

Jensen, L. "New Immigrant Settlements in Rural America: Problems, Prospects, and Policies." Durham: Carsey Institute, University of New Hampshire, 2006.

Jones, C. A., Kandel, W., and Parker, T. "Population Dynamics Are Changing the Profile of Rural Areas." *Amber Waves,* 2007, *5*(2), 30–35. Retrieved May 5, 2007, from http://www.ers.udsa.gov/AmberWaves/April07/Features/Population.htm.

Kelsey, T. W. *Fiscal Impacts of Different Land Uses: The Pennsylvania Experience.* University Park: Penn State College of Agricultural Sciences, 1997. Retrieved August 18, 2005, from http://cax.aers.psu.edu/localgovernment/Landuse.htm.

MacTavish, K., and Salamon, S. "What Do Rural Families Look Like Today?" In D. L. Brown and L. E. Swanson (eds.), *Challenges for Rural America in the Twenty-First Century.* University Park: Pennsylvania State University Press, 2003.

O'Toole, R. "Census Bureau: 94.6 Percent of U.S. Is Rural Open Space." *Environmental News,* July 1, 2003. Retrieved May 22, 2007, from http://www.heartland.org/Article.cfm?artId=12402.

Prensky, M. "Digital Natives, Digital Immigrants." Oct. 2001. Retrieved Aug. 20, 2007, from http://www.marcprensky.com/writing/Prensky%20-%20Digital%20Natives,%20Digital%20Immigrants%20-%20Part1.pdf.

Ritchey, J. A. *The Role of Religion in Shaping the Rural Context: A Study of a Small, Rural Community in Pennsylvania.* Lewiston, N.Y.: Edwin Mellen Press, 2002.

Ritchey, J. A. "Negotiating Change: Adult Education and Rural Life in Pennsylvania." *Pennsylvania Association for Adult Continuing Education Journal of Lifelong Learning,* 2006, *15,* 1–15.

Stone, K. E. "Impact of the Wal-Mart Phenomenon on Rural Communities." In *Proceedings of the National Public Policy Education Conference,* Charleston, S.C.: Sept. 21–24, 1997. Oak Brook, Ill.: Farm Foundation. Retrieved May 10, 2007, from http://www.farmfoundation.org/pubs/increas/97/contents.htm.

U.S. Department of Agriculture. Economic Research Service. "Measuring Rurality: What Is Rural?" 2007. Retrieved May 10, 2007, from http://www.ers.usda.gov/Briefing/Rurality/WhatisRural/.

Van Buren County Community Center. "What Is Rural Character?" 2003. Retrieved May 10, 2007, from http://www.vbco.org/planningeduc0059.asp.

Vidich, A. J. "Revolutions in Community Structure." In A. Gallaher and H. Padfield (eds.), *The Dying Community*. Albuquerque: University of New Mexico Press, 1980.

Whatmore, S. "On Doing Rural Research (or Breaking the Boundaries)." *Environment and Planning*, 1993, 25(5), 605–607.

JEFFREY A. RITCHEY is an assistant professor of adult and community education at Indiana University of Pennsylvania.

2

This chapter explores the relationship between popular education and the grassroots community-based educational principles of the Cooperative Extension Service's programs, which are grounded in the Progressive period and effectively used today in community economic development.

Extension and Community: The Practice of Popular and Progressive Education

Jeff Zacharakis

Although most articles and chapters on the Cooperative Extension Service (CES) begin with its early history and focus on its development from an institutional or broad programmatic perspective (Applebee, 2000; Bruner and Yang, 1949; Prawl, Medlin, and Gross, 1984; Rasmussen, 1989), this chapter examines the relationship between community economic development and popular education. It shows how CES's educational principles are historically grounded in the Progressive period and that this foundation continues to offer opportunities for creative programming and critical thinking that seeks to strengthen our democracy by engaging everyday people in a democratic process. Finally, I make the argument that in spite of a complex organizational and bureaucratic structure, the CES has active groups of educators who should be recognized as popular educators working for democratic social change toward a more equitable society.

The CES's historical roots in land grant universities are connected to rural agriculture and rural people, yet today's Extension programming is a mere reflection of what it was fifty years ago. It has grown into a complex bureaucracy that has taken on a life of its own, connected to yet separate from the land grant mission and connected to yet separate from rural people and agriculture, employing over seventeen thousand professional staff and faculty and tens of thousands of volunteers, permeating all aspects of rural and urban society. As an educational organization that serves all communities, urban, suburban, and rural, extension comprises over sixty

NEW DIRECTIONS FOR ADULT AND CONTINUING EDUCATION, no. 117, Spring 2008 © 2008 Wiley Periodicals, Inc.
Published online in Wiley InterScience (www.interscience.wiley.com) • DOI: 10.1002/ace.282

national program areas and a multitude of local programs that are initiated at state, county, and community levels. It is not easy or fair to characterize extension as one unified and monolithic organization. Rather it is a complex set of organizations that are shaped by many factors; each has a local flavor, and each also fits under a national umbrella. It is arguably the largest adult education organization in the United States. Like many other large bureaucracies, the CES employs people who do not have a progressive organizational vision and are content to conduct business as they did from their first day on the job. The CES also employs many energetic individuals who are arguably some of the nation's most dynamic and committed advocates of civil society and social change.

My inspiration for writing this chapter stems from my eleven years as a community developer for Iowa State University Extension and my ongoing work with extension at Kansas State University. After working seven years as a member of the Lindeman Center at Northern Illinois University, I became an area community development specialist for Iowa State University Extension. The multidisciplinary group I worked with consisted of ten area specialists who were located around the state, serving eight to twelve counties each. In addition, our team included about fourteen faculty members from the departments of sociology, economics, political science, community and regional planning, and civil engineering. This group varied not only by discipline but also by perspective and personality. Some might be categorized as fiscal conservatives and others social liberals; some were technicians, while others were visionaries or idea people. This diversity in our team was its strength. In essence, we were a theory-to-practice organization with a strong collective perspective of servicing Iowa's communities and people. Through this experience, I developed a passion for extension's mission and an understanding of its complexity, importance, and potential.

Extension Today

When the term *extension* is used today, it refers to the CES. The CES is a national, publicly funded, nonformal educational system that links the educational and research resources and activities of the U.S. Department of Agriculture (USDA) with over one hundred land grant institutions in every state, territory, and the District of Columbia. The CES has offices staffed with full-time professionals in almost every county and parish. This complex partnership focuses on providing research-based information on practical everyday problems that citizens from all walks of life in every community encounter. The federal partner of the CES is the Cooperative State Research, Education and Extension Service (CSREES), an agency of the USDA whose mission is to unite research, higher education, and extension education with the USDA's outreach resources and to advance knowledge of agriculture, the environment, human health and well-being, and communities.

New Directions for Adult and Continuing Education • DOI: 10.1002/ace

The state partnership of the CES is primarily housed in every state's land grant university, each having a mission statement that varies from state to state and from institution to institution. At the University of Wisconsin, extension's mission is to provide a portal to the university so "all Wisconsin people can access university resources and engage in lifelong learning, wherever they live and work" (University of Wisconsin–Extension, n.d., p. 1). The mission of Texas A&M's Extension Service is to "provide quality, relevant outreach and continuing education programs and services to the people of Texas" (Texas Cooperative Extension Agency, n.d., p. 1), and Oregon State University Extension "engages the people of Oregon with research-based knowledge and education that focus on strengthening communities and economies, sustaining natural resources, and promoting healthy families and individuals" (Oregon State University, n.d., p. 1). These three examples are representative of the country's land grant extension programs. Universally the CES seeks to make available university resources to develop relevant programs to meet the needs of all people in their homes, communities, and places of work. Its mission is ambitious and can easily be criticized at times for not having enough focus.

The programming principles for the CES embody the concepts of needs-based education, collaborative learning, learning by doing, and lifelong learning. From the beginning, extension promoted program development based on the needs, concerns, and problems of individuals and communities. These programs were developed *with* people, not *for* people, and were based on a thorough analysis of the facts relevant to particular situations. This approach was in contrast to developing a universal program that could be replicated across the country and designed to contribute to greater local cooperation, coordination, and efficiency. Finally, extension's programming has always embodied adult education's teaching-learning process, where the goal is not to tell people what to do but to teach them how to solve their problems and learn from others who have had similar problems (Prawl, Medlin, and Gross, 1984). Inherent in these principles is the belief that education needs to be problem based, where the scientific method can be applied to develop solutions that reflect collaboration between the community and the university or college. Citizens not only need to be involved in identifying problems but also included as integral participants in developing solutions and applying strategies. Although the expert model still underlies many of extension's programs—as characterized by professional university researchers—in most programs, citizens are seen as collegial co-researchers and co-experts.

Extension as Shaped by Its Progressive History

Historically extension's mission has had a pervasive rural and proletariat theme. Its original goal was to help "rural families help themselves by applying science, whether physical or social, to the daily routines of farming, homemaking, and family and community living" (Bruner and Yang, 1949, p. 1). There has been much written on the roots of extension, extending back to George Washington's first speech to Congress, when he called for a national university with an agricultural department that would diffuse information to farmers. Washington's vision to bring applied education to rural areas continued to grow throughout the early nineteenth century at a time when higher education in the United States was designed for elite and other privileged people. This level of education was not readily available to most working-class and rural people until the passage of the Morrill Act in 1862, which established the land grant university system, and the Second Morrill Act in 1890, which expanded the land grant system to include historically black universities. The Second Morrill Act was an appropriations bill that provided federal support for existing land grant colleges. It forbade racial discrimination in admissions, but states were allowed to escape this provision if separate institutions were maintained (Herren and Edwards, 2002). Hence, separate but equal racial politics led to the creation of the 1890 land grant schools. The two Morrill Acts represent the first comprehensive legislation to establish in each state a federally funded structure to provide higher education for all people. Rasmussen (1989) argued that the establishment of the land grant system created the opportunity for knowledge to "be made available to those not attending those institutions and should continue to be available throughout one's life. Thus was the university brought to the people" (p. 3).

In order to receive land allotments and federal funds, each state had to provide education and training in agriculture and mechanic arts (engineering), while creating an applied vision of higher education. By targeting rural populations, extension fostered a populist vision of education, recognizing that rural communities and farmers were facing not only economic issues of poverty but also health and nutrition problems that affected their overall quality of life. Rural agriculture and applied knowledge became synonymous with the land grant system at a time when most of the country's population was rural and farming was primarily a small, family enterprise. In the late twentieth century, American Indian tribes argued that their reservations were the only areas not to participate in the land grant system. In 1994, the land grant system expanded to include tribal colleges in twelve states whose mission is primarily to serve American Indians. This legislation not only included federal funds for the tribal colleges but also resources to support collaboration with the rest of the land grant system (Herren and Edwards, 2002).

The CES, established by the Smith-Lever Act in 1914, was created to provide a formal structure for rural and agricultural education. The goal of this legislation was to make "rural life profitable, healthful, comfortable, and attractive" (Rasmussen, 1989, p. 48). The history of extension is steeped in a utopian vision of creating a more equitable and profitable life for rural Americans. To understand the birth of extension, one needs to understand its relationship to the Progressive movement in the early twentieth century, a period when women earned the right to vote, senators became elected in lieu of appointment, regulations and antitrust legislation were created to control big business and corporate corruption, child labor laws were passed, and national parks were created to protect natural resources and pristine areas.

Progressives such as John Dewey, Jane Addams, Kenyon Butterfield, and Edward Lindeman emerged as voices that ushered in modern adult education and also shaped the vision for extension. These luminaries saw education as the way to create a stronger and more equitable society. Addams (1902) urged politicians and decision makers to invest more in education: "It is at last on behalf of the average workingmen that our increasing democracy impels us to make a new demand upon the educator" (p. 192). Dewey and Dewey (1915) might have best argued for this education that would enable all to participate in the emerging democratic spirit of the Progressive period: "The democracy which proclaims equality of opportunity as its ideal requires an education in which learning and social application, ideas and practice, work and recognition of the meaning of what is done, are united from the beginning and for all" (p. 315).

Lindeman (1989) furthered the Progressive connection to adult education that was embedded in extension's core values by setting forth four broad precepts on adult education: the "whole of life is learning, therefore education can have no endings" (p. 4), it is "conceived as process conterminous with life" (p. 5), "the approach to adult education will be via the route of situations, not subjects" (p. 6), and "the resource of highest value in adult education is the learner's experience" (p. 6). Education for all people, not just children, was seen by Progressives as the best way to solve social ills and modernize American society.

Extension grew out of this Progressive period to be, as Butterfield (1932) argued, "probably the most elaborate project in rural adult education in the world . . . not only the most extensive and popular system of rural adult education which we are likely to have, but that it is capable of carrying a goodly share in the new developments that may be found necessary and practical" (p. 494). Bruner and Yang (1946) described the grass-roots, democratic approach of extension's programming during its early years. They pointed out that because extension was connected to each state's land grant university and had offices in every county, it had the ability to be flexible and tailor its programs to the needs of the specific group or community through the county agent.

Once extension was established locally, rural people in particular grew to trust and request assistance when problems arose. This problem-centered approach often meant that different solutions had to be developed for each problem, in lieu of national solutions dictated by Washington, D.C. Just as various regions in the country differed and local variables changed, extension evolved as a flexible organization able to develop educational programming that reflected local issues and needs. Its approach was educational, which implied that county agents and university professors did not fix problems but rather developed demonstrations and worked with local citizens to find solutions to problems. An educational environment was created where people with similar problems could meet one another while attending a demonstration, sharing what they knew and developing new networks with their peers.

During the Progressive period, there was a common goal among many leaders and within many civic institutions to strengthen democratic society along a populist ideology. Extension during this period strongly believed in its mission to strengthen rural people, communities, and economies through collectives and cooperatives, a process not too dissimilar from the same evolution that was occurring in unions. During the 1920s, extension had educational programs to promote the formation of cooperatives and show how they might lead to greater economic independence for farmers, families, and rural businesses. These programs helped spur the exponential growth of cooperative organizations and membership prior to the Great Depression (Brunner and Wang, 1949).

Throughout the Great Depression in the 1930s, extension worked with farmers to develop an agricultural relief program where farmers approved of crop and production controls to prevent overproduction and lower prices. Getting farmers to explore limiting production collectively was a high-risk initiative in the light of their lack of networks and organizations. Analyzing problems and developing solutions in collaboration with citizens resulted in a form of political action that characterized many of extension's early programs (Brunner and Wang, 1949). Another example of extension's work that exemplifies its Progressive mission for rural people occurred in the late 1930s and early 1940s, when it developed programs to address economic and health problems affecting black southern adults (Washington, 1939; McAllister and McAllister, 1945). At a time when segregation was the rule and rural poverty was at its worst in the South, extension developed home and farm demonstration programs for rural black farmers and families that were designed not only as a systematic form of instruction, but also as "an attack in the natural setting on real-life problems, the solutions of which are absolutely essential for social and economic well-being. The [extension] program [was] designed to change ideals, attitudes and conduct of individuals so that the rural people will achieve a better life" (McAllister and McAllister, 1945, p. 331). Extension's mission to extend education beyond the classroom and to provide scientific information was the same regardless of whether the group was black or white. At a time when there were few university resources available to rural black communities, extension was one of the few institutions with programs designed to address issues specific to these communities.

Kreitlow (1973) argued that extension educators should be willing to test their security and take proactive roles in controversial programs and issues. He pointed out that extension "in the early days thrived on grass-roots programming and participant involvement" (p. 13) but was unfortunately evolving into an organization with more specialists pursuing security in an expert educational model. This tension between being a locally centered, grassroots model and a university-based expert model still exists within extension, and some might even argue that this tension is healthy. What initially gave extension credibility, and what still gives it credibility, is that the majority of its programs have emerged from community needs. As Kreitlow pointed out, excitement and energy have always been generated by extension educators willing to test their security.

Although extension was established as a federal-state cooperative agreement, its history is steeped in the Progressive period reflecting populist ideals. Out of this foundation emerged creative and effective programs that sought to improve the lives of farmers and impoverished rural communities. While some of these high-risk programs may not have been successful or met their goals, numerous examples illustrate extension's historical willingness to venture into controversial topics and programs in order to achieve its mission.

Connecting Extension to Popular Education

Although there is not one definition for popular education that fits all situations, it has the basic tenets of horizontal relationships between the educator or facilitator and the group or community. Popular education also responds to a community or group's need and requires that they be full participants in planning and implementation. Most important, popular education "acknowledges that the community is the source of knowledge" (Hamilton and Cunningham, 1991, p. 443). The historical tradition within popular education is to promote social change through education and create a dialogue among the disenfranchised, as well as with society at large, concerning the political strategies necessary to eliminate social inequality. Popular education originated in Latin America (Choules, 2007) within a postcolonial, third world context as characterized by Freire's *Pedagogy of the Oppressed* (1970). And while concerns have been expressed about the effectiveness of Freirean education in Western, developed countries such as the United States (Facundo, 1984; Zacharakis-Jutz, 1988), clearly there are exploited and oppressed groups and communities within these societies. Granted, not all community development is popular education, yet most popular education arguably is community work that seeks social change. This is especially true within adult education, where "community development traditionally has sought social change in an evolutionary manner, as compared with a revolutionary agenda for popular education" (Hamilton and Cunningham, 1991, p. 446).

If social change can be universally accepted as a key component of that intersection between community development and popular education, there

are many examples within extension's community development programming that fall within this definition of popular education. Recently the CES
has worked closely with small farmers as part of the national movement to
create community-supported agriculture (CSA). CSA offers farmers the
opportunity to sell their produce and meats locally at farmers' markets and
directly to consumers through subscriptions where individuals and families
buy shares of a farm's production. It is a marketing strategy that eliminates
brokers and middlemen while offering the freshest and often the highest-
quality product to the consumer. Extension in almost every state has been
a key stakeholder in this movement by providing expertise in starting small
businesses; sponsoring conferences, farm tours, and workshops; and con-
ducting test plots with different varieties of vegetables and other produce
(Abel, Thomson, and Maretzke, 1999; Gradwell, 1997; Sharp, Imerman, and
Peters, 2002). Extension provides educational support on topics like food
safety, preparing fresh foods, and, most important, creating bridges between
producers and consumers. At a time when most of our food is produced on
large, commercial farms and sold directly to corporations for processing,
these large enterprises depend very little on the local community for supplies and technical assistance. Extension's work with small- and medium-
sized farms enhances the viability of local communities, where they both
buy supplies and sell their products. This initiative is akin to the formation
of collectives and cooperatives in the 1920s.

Another initiative that is gaining momentum and is supported strongly
in many states by the CES is the economic development strategy for developing local economies (Flora and Flora, 1993; Johnson, 1989; Scorsone,
2003). In the Midwest and High Plains, as well as many other areas in the
country, communities are seeing population losses (and in particular a brain
drain as the best and brightest youth leave for greener pastures), school con-
solidations, small business closings, and the decline of civic institutions and
services. Fallacious dreams of attracting new automobile plants or prisons
to these communities seldom materialize. More and more rural economists
are arguing that a more realistic strategy is needed to support local entrepreneurship. "Entrepreneurship is the new focal point for rural development. This was the consensus of two hundred rural policy officials and
experts who gathered in Kansas City, April 28–29, 2003, for the fourth
annual rural policy conference hosted by the Federal Reserve Banks of
Kansas City" (Drabenstott, Novack, and Abraham, 2003, p. 1).

In 1995, while working for Iowa State University Extension, I was part
of a team that developed a program entitled Quality Jobs for Quality Communities. In selected communities, we held a series of town meetings with
local leaders and residents to show how investing in their community financially and programmatically could strengthen the community's sustainability. The first stage of this project was to "generate grass roots interest in and
discussion on the topic of quality jobs" (Iowa State University Extension,
n.d., p. 1). Many of these communities never considered what a "quality

job" was; rather they would market their communities to prospective out-side employers by trying to sell their average low wages as an asset—wages so low that often two and even three jobs were required just to raise the household above the poverty level. Following these town meetings, several participating communities agreed to study and analyze this problem, which resulted in strategies where they would invest more in developing their own economy and jobs through entrepreneurial activities, in contrast to the fail-ing strategy of recruiting new jobs from other locations across the country. This in part meant educating community banks on the benefits of making loans to local entrepreneurs, which previously in Iowa was not considered compatible with local conservative banking practices.

In 1993, North Carolina A&T State University offered another grass-roots program, entitled Community Voices: Leadership Development for Community Decision-Making. In this participatory educational program, extension staff worked with existing leaders to identify key stakeholder groups in the community. They in turn identified, recruited, and groomed new and emerging leaders. Together they began to build a collective vision of what they wanted their community to be in five or ten years, based on the premise that in order for a community to move forward, everyone had to be at the table and develop a shared commitment to work together over a long period of time. The primary outcomes of this program were to mobi-lize the entire community toward the creation and implementation of a community and economic development strategic plan.

Popular Education Within Extension

Every popular education project begins with dialogue at a grassroots level. For the CES, this dialogue is possible only because of the relationship that the CES's county agents, community developers, faculty, and staff have with each community. Land grant universities are the only higher education insti-tutions where professional staff work and live in almost every county in their state. The results of this arrangement are twofold. First, the university has an agent who can listen and respond to the needs of many communities and groups, and second, the community has a conduit to the university through which it can lobby for resources. This relationship is highly polit-ical and thus strengthens the mission of land grant universities. When it is working, state legislators hear from their constituents, who demand that funding be maintained for the university. And when it is not working, uni-versity presidents are asked by these same legislators, "What have you done for my communities?" While no one claims that all of the CES's community development programs embody popular education or are effective in creat-ing social change toward a more democratic society, there are many exam-ples of popular education programs offered through the CES. It may seem to be a contradiction to have institutionalized popular education programs, but this interlocking network of county, state, and federal organizations is essential to ensure that extension's participatory mission and programming are stronger and more sustainable than any one organization or individual could hope to maintain.

In July 1988, I was part of a group of sixty adult educators who met in Leeds, England, to discuss how adult educators could create social change through their research and practice. Out of this dialogue emerged a vision and network that would be called "transformative research" (Beder, 1991, p. 3). Transformative research is research that is centered in ethical, emancipatory, empowering, and holistic values, addressing issues related to human rights, social justice, oppression, and disadvantaged groups (Deshler and Selener, 1991). During one session, a colleague demonstrated how we might seek cracks within universities in which to push and expand opportunities for popular education and transformative research. Extension has many cracks and many opportunities for popular educators to grow and blossom professionally as social change agents.

References

Abel, J., Thomson, J., and Maretzki, A. "Extension's Role with Farmers' Markets: Working with Farmers, Consumers, and Communities." *Journal of Extension,* 1999, *37*(5). Retrieved April 5, 2007, from http://www.joe.org/joe/1999october/a4.html.

Addams, J. *Democracy and Social Ethics.* New York: Macmillan, 1902.

Applebee, G. J. "Cooperative Extension." In A. L. Wilson and E. R. Hayes (eds.), *Handbook of Adult and Continuing Education.* San Francisco: Jossey-Bass, 2000.

Beder, H. "Mapping the Terrain." *Convergence,* 1991, *24*(3), 3–8.

Bruner, E., and Yang, E.H.P. *Rural America and the Extension Service.* New York: Teachers College, Columbia University, 1949.

Butterfield, K. L. "Some Rural Aspects of Adult Education." *Journal of Educational Sociology,* 1932, *5*(8), 493–499.

Choules, K. "Social Change Education: Context Matters." *Adult Education Quarterly,* 2007, *57*(2), 159–176.

Deshler, D., and Selener, D. "Transformative research: In search of definition." *Convergence,* 1991, *24*(3), 9–23.

Dewey, J., and Dewey, E. *Schools of Tomorrow.* New York: Dutton, 1915.

Drabenstott, M., Novack, N., and Abraham, B. "Main Streets of Tomorrow: Growing and Financing Rural Entrepreneurs." Kansas City: Federal Reserve Banks of Kansas City, 2003. Retrieved Apr. 5, 2007, from http://econpapers.repec.org/article/fipfedkms/.

Facundo, B. *Issues for an Evaluation of Freire-Inspired Programs in the United States and Puerto Rico.* 1984. (ED 243 998)

Flora, C. B., and Flora, J. "Entrepreneurial Social Infrastructure: A Necessary Ingredient." *Annals of the American Academy of Political and Social Science,* 1993, *529,* 48–58.

Freire, P. *Pedagogy of the Oppressed.* New York: Continuum, 1970.

Gradwell, S. *Iowa Community Supported Agriculture Guide for Producers and Organizers.* Ames: Iowa State University Extension, 1997.

Hamilton, D., and Cunningham, P. M. "Community-Based Adult Education." In S. B. Merriam and P. M. Cunningham (eds.), *Handbook of Adult and Continuing Education.* San Francisco: Jossey-Bass, 1991.

Herren, R. V., and Edwards, M. C. "Whence We Came: The Land-Grant Tradition— Origin, Evolution, and Implications for the 21st Century." *Journal of Agricultural Education,* 2002, *43*(4), 88–98.

Iowa State University Extension. "Quality Jobs for Quality Communities, Project Stages." n.d. Retrieved Apr. 20, 2007, from http://www.extension.iastate.edu/qualityjobs/stages.html.

Johnson, T. G. "Entrepreneurship and Development Finance: Keys to Rural Revitalization Discussion." *American Journal of Agricultural Economics*, 1989, 71(5), 1324–1326.

Kreitlow, B. W. "Controversy: Its Positive Role in Education." *Journal of Extension*, 1973, 11(3), 9–16. Retrieved Mar. 22, 2007, from www.joe.org/joe/1973=3=a1.pdf.

Lindeman, E. C. *The Meaning of Adult Education*. Norman: University of Oklahoma, 1989. (Original work published 1926)

McAllister, J. E., and McAllister, D. M. "Adult Education for Negroes in Rural Areas: The Work of the Jeanes Teachers and Home and Farm Demonstration Agents." *Journal of Negro Education*, 1945, 14(3), 331–340.

Oregon State University. "Mission and Vision." N.d. Retrieved Apr. 25, 2007, from http://extension.oregonstate.edu/admin/mission.php.

Prawl, W., Medlin, R., and Gross, J. *Adult and Continuing Education Through the Cooperative Extension Service*. Columbia: Extension Division, University of Missouri, 1984.

Rasmussen, W. D. *Taking the University to the People: Seventy-Five Years of Cooperative Extension*. Ames: Iowa State University Press, 1989.

Scorsone, E. "Encouraging Entrepreneurship in Rural Communities: The University of Kentucky Entrepreneurship Initiative Program." *Journal of Extension*, 2003, 41(6). Retrieved May 2, 2007, from http://www.joe.org/joe/2003december/iw5.shtml.

Sharp, J., Imerman, E., and Peters, G. "Community Supported Agriculture: Building Community Among Farmers and Non-Farmers." *Journal of Extension*, 2002, 40(3).

Texas Cooperative Extension Agency. "Mission." N.d. Retrieved Apr. 25, 2007, from http://agextension.tamu.edu/mission.htm.

University of Wisconsin-Extension. "Select Mission." N.d. Retrieved May 2, 2007, from http://www.uwex.edu/about/mission/.

Washington, A. H. "Rural Education—The Cooperative Movement." *Journal of Negro Education*, 1939, 8(1), 104–111.

Zacharakis-Jutz, J. "Post-Freirean Adult Education: A Question of Empowerment and Power." *Adult Education Quarterly*, 1988, 39(1), 41–47.

JEFF ZACHARAKIS is an assistant professor in the Department of Educational Leadership and an associate of the Institute for Civic Discourse and Democracy at Kansas State University.

3

Legislation over the past two decades has shaped the dominant view of adult literacy as addressing gaps in well-defined, measurable skills. As rural communities face unprecedented challenges, this one-size-fits-all view of adult literacy does not consider the unique local context of rural communities or involve those communities in defining their own needs and goals.

Rural Adult Literacy in a Community Context: From the Margin to the Mainstream

Mary F. Ziegler, Dent C. Davis

Rural communities have historically faced different challenges from their urban counterparts, lagging behind in access to health care, education, career opportunities, and communication (Gibbs, 2003, 2005). However, as population trends shift and technology ushers in new forms of work, rural areas are changing. Some rural communities with natural resources are growing because of the urban demand for recreational areas or retirement sites. Other rural communities have seen a major increase in population because of international migration. In contrast, some rural populations are declining, particularly where loss of industry to overseas competitors has forced young families to look for opportunities elsewhere (U.S. Department of Agriculture, 1997). Overall, economic and educational opportunities and resources in rural communities continue to lag behind those of urban areas (Gibbs, 2004). Concern for rural America is real. Although rural areas contribute to goods and services, the concerns go beyond economics. "Rural America is also home to a fifth of the Nation's people, keeper of natural amenities and national treasures, and safeguard of a unique part of American culture, tradition, and history" (U.S. Department of Agriculture, 1997, p. 1). Rural communities are addressing their challenges in different ways, and in many cases, innovative learning opportunities are a part of those strategies. Such opportunities invite a view of adult literacy that takes into consideration the local context. One approach for considering local context is through building social capital.

NEW DIRECTIONS FOR ADULT AND CONTINUING EDUCATION, no. 117, Spring 2008 © 2008 Wiley Periodicals, Inc.
Published online in Wiley InterScience (www.interscience.wiley.com) • DOI: 10.1002/ace.283

Social capital focuses on "collective norms of reciprocity and mutual trust that link people together in ways that enable them to solve problems and work together for the common good" (Ewert and Grace, 2000, p. 333). Social capital has long been associated with rural contexts (Parks, Kennedy, and Placenti, 2000). Despite their noteworthy differences, many rural communities continue to exhibit greater social capital than do urban communities (Parks, Kennedy, and Placenti, 2000), a factor that offers promise for contributing to broad stakeholder participation in community initiatives (Capagrossi, Ewert, Deshler, and Greene, 1994; Quigley, 2005).

Traditional forms of community development have focused on economic and human capital. Economic capital focuses on financial resources invested in a community to affect productivity. Human capital focuses on the development of individual skills and abilities also related to productivity. Both economic and human capital have dominated approaches to adult literacy education and community development in recent decades (Ewert and Grace, 2000). Portes (1998) describes the difference among economic, human, and social capital: ". . . Whereas economic capital is in people's bank accounts and human capital is inside their heads, social capital inheres in the structure of their relationships" (p. 7). Networks, relationships, and trust are the currency of social capital, and the resulting social cohesion becomes a critical resource for ongoing learning and development in the community. Fostering inclusive participation and a broad base of leadership builds social capital while often strengthening economic and human capital.

This chapter shows how these various forms of capital are interconnected in a local effort to use education to protect and enliven a rural community's future. In this chapter, we describe a rural community in southern Appalachia and the work of a diverse group from all sectors of the community who developed a partnership to strengthen adult literacy (which they called basic skills) as part of community development. The project extended over five years and involved strengthening participation in a community-wide partnership focused on basic skills as a part of community development. Although unique to the local context, lessons learned from this project may be valuable for adult educators who are working with rural communities to strengthen adult literacy. We begin by describing the county, its educational programs, and the development of the partnership. Next, we note the lessons learned, and finally we address the potential applications of this story for other adult literacy efforts in rural areas.

Restin County Story

Restin County (a pseudonym) is located in southern Appalachia, seventy-five miles from the nearest metropolitan center and thirty miles by two-lane road from the nearest interstate highway. The county has five municipal areas and a population of approximately forty thousand individuals in more

New Directions for Adult and Continuing Education • DOI: 10.1002/ace

than fifteen thousand households. Only eleven companies located in the county employ fifty or more individuals. Unemployment is approximately 10 percent. With a per capita income of fifteen thousand dollars, as much as 15 percent of the population is below the poverty line. Approximately 60 percent of adults aged twenty-five years and over have a high school diploma or its equivalent. The number of those who did not graduate from high school is approximately 25 percent higher than the state average (U.S. Census Bureau, 2000; U.S. Department of Labor, 2007).

As in many other rural counties, the adult basic education program in Restin County consisted of one full-time program manager-teacher and a part-time teacher who were employees of the local school system. Following the public school calendar, the program focused on preparing adults for the general education development (GED) examination. Adults enrolled in classes that were held in a building near the local high school. Because instruction was individualized, teachers relied on workbooks from major publishing companies. The nearest community college was thirty miles away, and the nearest four-year college was an additional twenty-five miles. The adult basic education staff were affiliated with the local school system but worked independently to implement their classes. Occasionally they interacted with local school representatives or the local librarian. They had little contact with other organizations in the community and no formal affiliations.

The adult basic education program was isolated. Although the program staff had relationships with individuals from other agencies, there was no structure in place that promoted interaction. Like other programs that provided social services, they reported directly to the state offices that provided funding. Accountability was at the state and federal levels rather than at the local level. Educational program and social service agency staff had little reason or incentive to interact with local business or industry. The lack of communication or coordination among different stakeholder groups in the county was not apparent in day-to-day activities. At the same time, the county was experiencing a rapid decline. A combination of industrial plant closings, lack of population growth, an aging population, low educational levels, and diminishing financial resources had combined with the county's geographical remoteness to produce a decline in the vitality of the area. There were fewer employers, jobs, and qualified applicants for the jobs that were available. Young families were leaving the county for opportunities elsewhere.

Experiencing this problem firsthand, a local director of training who was active in the community decided to engage other local leaders from business and education in a conversation to address the county's future. This gathering led to many other meetings and an eventual decision to open the conversation to the broader community. A small group of volunteers organized an open meeting at a local utility company. They were surprised at the attendance and even more so at the broad cross-section of people who wanted to be involved and contribute ideas. A key outcome of the meeting was acknowledgment of the need for stronger basic skills for community members, particularly those who did not graduate from high school or wanted to prepare themselves for postsecondary education. In addition, all those at the meeting believed that there was a universal need for basic skills in the use of information technology.

That meeting was the beginning of the development of the Community Learning Network, a local public-private partnership to increase learning opportunities in the county that would lead to economic and community development. At the beginning of the partnership, the goals of the Community Learning Network were not focused, and resources were sparse. However, there was a group of people from a broad cross-section of the community committed to this effort, and they contributed their time and even some resources because they thought that a local partnership network could make a difference.

In early meetings, the emerging network identified key stakeholder groups in the county, including citizens, government agencies, the local adult basic education program, and businesses. Initial partnership activities involved numerous meetings where individuals discussed the future of the county, its strengths and weaknesses, and ways to build its capacity. Early on, the growing network of partners decided they needed additional data about the educational needs of the county.

Local leaders and representatives from various segments of the community created and administered two surveys to determine the kinds of knowledge and skills needed for the future. As adult educational consultants, our role was to facilitate a collaborative process for developing and administering the surveys, analyzing the data, reporting to the community, and facilitating follow-up activities. The first survey was for local residents; it involved members of the community in the design of the questions and dozens of volunteers who distributed and collected more than six hundred surveys at public sites throughout the county. The survey asked residents what skills they had and which they would like to improve, including basic skills such as reading, writing, and working with numbers. There were questions about other skills, such as using technology, communication, and teamwork. The survey asked how people liked to learn, for example, in formal classes, on the job, or on their own. Additional questions asked how supportive the community was of their learning needs. The second survey was for seventeen local businesses and included an analysis of organizational learning needs (Davis and Ziegler, 1995). It was administered to fifteen hundred employees from a variety of organizations, including manufacturing companies, a local utility company, a newspaper, and a police department representing the county's municipal areas. Specific questions about work-related basic skills were part of this survey. In addition, we conducted interviews with employees at all levels of the organization and asked about the ways that learning occurred and how it could be more effective.

The survey results of the local residents indicated a keen interest in learning, including basic skills and other skills related to their work and family roles. However, there was a perceived lack of opportunity for learning in the community. The surveys of employees in the local businesses showed that there were common training and education needs, including training in collaboration and teamwork, skills using information technology, and the need for work-related basic skills.

The results of these surveys were reported to approximately fifty members of the Community Learning Network who gathered at a state park in the county. Around the table at that meeting sat a wide variety of participants: the mayor; council members; business owners; plant managers; company training directors; representatives from the library, community college, local adult basic education program, and police, fire, and sanitation departments; local and state economic development professionals; representatives from the public school system; participants in adult learning programs; volunteers; and interested citizens. A common theme of the meeting was a strong sense of the fundamental importance of increasing educational opportunities, particularly basic skills, as a path to higher-wage jobs and increased community health and vitality. Discussion focused on the community's primary concern that industry was leaving the area, forcing families to look for work outside the county. Information from the meeting was published in the local paper, generating further interest in the work of the network.

This gathering of community stakeholders served as an important turning point: it led the Community Learning Network to undertake a number of activities over the next several years that crossed traditional boundaries. There were additional collaborative efforts among public and private sector partners. As the goals of the network became clearer through collaboration, the community was able to secure grants that helped to fund a community learning center that included state-of-the-art information technology resources. This provided a physical space where network partners collaborated to provide a variety of education and training events. Regular adult basic education classes were offered in the center to different groups, and the community college in the area opened an office in the same location to explore distance education. All programs had greater visibility and more cross-over. Participation in adult basic education increased, and this led to more exposure to other public training and education opportunities. Members volunteered to organize and conduct collaborative learning activities identified by the community surveys such as team training for small businesses. As the story of Restin County spread, other counties sought information about this effort. Local Restin County representatives from various sectors became involved in regional and state partnership efforts. These contacts enabled the county to access additional funding and resources for education, community, and economic development.

The network began more than ten years ago with a vision for the community's future. Some of the changes that have occurred in the community are noteworthy. Residents have seen an increase in pathways into educational opportunities, and education and learning have been slowly integrated into a broader community context. However, there continue to be challenges. Although three new industries have come to the county, an accomplishment attributed to the network, two plants have closed. While educational opportunities have increased for county residents, the number of available high-quality jobs has not met expectations. Grant funding is less available and more competitive. Support from state and federal government is affected by fewer resources and greater competition for resources from other rural communities. The community is facing these challenges by continuing to strengthen partnerships that cross traditional boundaries. In today's rapidly changing world, these types of partnership networks can serve as catalysts for learning, and especially for adult literacy, as learning moves from the margin to the mainstream.

Lessons Learned

Restin County is unique but shares many of the challenges faced by other rural communities that are linking adult literacy and basic skills to community development. Although the Community Learning Network began as a response to a need for economic and human capital development, what has sustained the community was the increase in social capital created by formalizing relationships in the network. The lessons learned from this project include the importance of relationships, partnerships as a way to structure relationships, the value of broad participation, social capital as a way to conceive collaborative relationships, and learning as the foundation for both program development and program content.

Relationships. A key to effective community development in today's world involves changing the nature of social relationships (Korten, 1990). Effective relationships are increasingly seen as an asset in educational program development as well as economic and community development. Social cohesion has long been associated with rural communities (Parks, Kennedy, and Placenti, 2000). Although cohesion is often high in rural communities, the cohesion is not necessarily structured in such a way that it leads to overall gains for the community. People may know each other but not cross work or social boundaries. A collaborative process creates a structure for the community to harness the social cohesion for a mutually beneficial goal. As they work together, they may cross social boundaries because community residents in different social roles, at different economic levels, and with different literacy levels may be working on the same project and learning from one another.

Partnerships. A way to formalize relationships is by forming partnerships. Partnerships might be conceived as intentional, systematic approaches to enhancing social capital in local communities. Effective partnerships among individuals and groups focus on specific goals through

New Directions for Adult and Continuing Education • DOI: 10.1002/ace

cooperation, collaboration, and shared responsibility. For example, partnerships can have a positive effect on local adult basic education programs. As a result of the active participation of adult basic education program staff, participant referrals, financial support, and program visibility have the potential of increasing over time. In this way, adult basic education programs can meet their state goals and at the same time contribute to a larger literacy effort in the community. In Ewert and Grace's terms (2000), the program itself experienced an increase in its political, economic, and social capital. Community partnerships can strengthen local adult basic education programs and at the same time open complementary avenues for adult literacy that serve community and individual needs. By connecting with other individuals and groups in the community, learners may increase their access to opportunities otherwise unavailable to them.

Participation. Broad participation is the key to the effectiveness of a local community, a classroom experience, or a democracy. This project made the assumption that every member of the community was a potential participant and that it would be possible to bring multiple, and even competing, voices to the table. The Restin County experience underscored the assertion by scholars in the adult education and community development literature that participatory approaches to education and development are critical for effectiveness in rural environments (Capagrossi, Ewert, Deshler, and Greene, 1994; Quigley, 2005). Participants included leaders from the public and private sectors, educators, citizens, employees, and adult education program participants. As Sparks and Peterson (2000) note, "Too often missing from the discourse are the voices of those who ultimately determine the outcome of the program—the learners themselves" (p. 274). The diversity of participants in the network strengthened and enriched the partnership.

Although there was broad and effective participation in the network, there was no way to know if all stakeholder groups were adequately represented. Because of the distributed nature of the Community Learning Network, learning about effective strategies for stakeholder participation was ongoing and responsive to community input. An effective partnership needs to be transparent and public about its activities, particularly decision making, and to communicate these in a variety of ways. Regardless of the intentions of those involved, this is difficult to do when there are large numbers of stakeholders and stakeholder groups in different geographical locations. Sustained inclusivity and transparent decision making are an ongoing challenge among partners.

Social Capital. Social participation, or "collective action for mutual benefit" (Woolcock, 1998, p. 155), is one of the key assumptions of scholars who note the importance of social capital in rural community development initiatives. According to Ewert (1997), traditional approaches to adult basic education have tended to focus on the development of individual skills to enhance workplace productivity, an approach focusing on human

New Directions for Adult and Continuing Education • DOI: 10.1002/ace

capital. In contrast, traditional approaches to community development have focused on the investment of economic capital to increase productivity. The story of Restin County underscores Putnam's suggestion (1993) that there should be increased attention to the importance of social capital, or cooperation, mutual benefit, and networking, in developing programs that address not only adult literacy but also associated, locally identified needs. In the development of the Community Learning Network, Restin County's approach included emphasis on economic, human, and social capital. This can be seen, for example, in the creation of the community learning center, an outgrowth of the network. Economic capital from a wide variety of sources was invested in equipment designed to help participants increase their individual skills and productivity, a form of human capital. The center was conceived and developed as part of a collaborative effort that resulted in increased social capital because residents had broader connections with others in the community. Ewert (1997) suggests that economic, human, and social capital represent distinct ways of strengthening rural communities. Our experience in Restin County suggests that these forms of capital are not distinct; rather, they are intertwined and build on one another. Social capital may sustain a community even if the economic development does not occur as planned.

Learning at Multiple Levels. While such partnerships often have positive effects on local adult learning programs, the development of the network itself was also a learning process. There was no textbook to guide the network's development. The network evolved over time in response to a greater awareness of the needs of the community and available resources that could be obtained to support the effort. It began with a focus on economic development. Very quickly, however, participants in the partnership learned that community health and vitality required a larger vision with broader citizen involvement, better educational opportunities, attention to quality of life, and good communication across distances that have traditionally separated rural residents. Most of all, this health and vitality demanded the ability to adapt and learn in a rapidly changing and increasingly global environment. This learning involved an increased collective capacity on the part of network participants to work together to identify and address community issues. In ways similar to Finger and Asun's description (2001), participants had to "learn their way through" the problems as they built the network (p. 1). Horton and Freire (1990) described a similar process when they said, "We make the road by walking" (p. 6). The meaning of learning changes when people from diverse educational levels, social roles, or socioeconomic groups in a community collaborate. Although not all groups have the same decision-making authority, collaboration shifts the typical, more narrowly focused deficit view of adult literacy toward a broader conception of multiple literacies that are relevant for all residents regardless of their position. In such an environment, everyone becomes a learner.

New Directions for Adult and Continuing Education • DOI: 10.1002/ace

Developing effective adult literacy programs in rural communities is a learning process that takes time and requires resources. Trust among stakeholders must be earned, and it deepens as people believe their interests are included. Collaborative relationships take time to develop. In Restin County, it took more than three years for a broad base of partners to become active in the network. At the same time, federal legislation has limited the ability of local adult basic education programs to respond to local needs by imposing a national definition of basic skills and standard measurement criteria, that is, one size fits all (Ziegler and Bingman, 2007). "Historically literacy education in the U.S. has focused on individual needs not community problems" (Padamsee, Ewert, and Deshler, 1996, p. 2). Often there is a temptation to cut short the collaborative process in favor of obtaining short-term individual outcomes. The experience of Restin County suggests that longer-term attention to such strategies as local partnership development, along with the flexibility to meet local goals, holds promise for developing a greater capacity for long-term effectiveness. This echoes elements in the literature that underscore the importance of capacity building as a learning process in adult education program development (Lauzon, 2005). Local partnerships require learning similar to organizational learning approaches such as the learning organization (Senge, 1990) and the learning society (Jarvis, 2001). Tangible benefits help sustain the energy, commitment, and accountability that participation in community partnerships requires.

Conclusion

Effective literacy programs in rural communities require a heuristic approach to development and planning. Conceiving literacy as a lifelong learning effort that includes but extends beyond the GED makes literacy more relevant for the community at large. The story of Restin County points to the benefits of public-private partnerships in rural literacy education. ᵈʳessing the rapidity and scope of change in rural communities necessi- ˙ration. Local adult basic education programs do not have suf- ˙ources to meet the needs of multiple stakeholder groups County's experience suggests that partnership devel- ˙ective method for more broadly addressing rural

D., and Greene, J. *Literacy and Community* and Rural Development Institute, Cornell

ntification, Assessment and Implications of an e Practice of Adult Education in Organizational

New Directions for Adult and Continuing Education • DOI: 10.1002/ace

Settings." In P. Collette, B. Einsiedel, and S. Hobden (eds.), *Proceedings of the 36th Annual Adult Education Research Conference.* Edmonton, Alberta, Canada: University of Alberta, 1995.

Ewert, D. M. "Social Capital and Human Development." *Literacy Practitioner,* 1997, 4(2), 8, 12.

Ewert, D. M., and Grace, K. A. "Adult Education for Community Action." In A. L. Wilson and E. R. Hayes (eds.), *Handbook of Adult and Continuing Education.* San Francisco: Jossey-Bass, 2000.

Finger, M., and Asun, J. M. *Adult Education at the Crossroads: Learning Our Way Out.* New York: ZED Books, 2001.

Gibbs, R. "Rural Education at a Glance." 2003. USDA Economic Research Service. Retrieved Nov. 20, 2006, from http://www.ers.usda.gov/publications/rdrr98/ rdrr98 _lowres.pdf.

Gibbs, R. "Rural Income, Poverty, and Welfare: Overview." 2004. USDA Economic Research Service. Retrieved Nov. 20, 2006, from http://www.ers.usda.gov/Briefing/ IncomePovertyWelfare/Overview.htm.

Gibbs, R. "Education as a Rural Development Strategy." *Amber Waves,* 2005, 3(5), 20–25. Retrieved Nov. 20, 2006, from http://www.ers.usda.gov/AmberWaves/November05/ pdf/FeatureEducationNovember2005.pdf.

Horton, M., and Freire, P. *We Make the Road by Walking: Conversations on Education and Social Change.* Philadelphia: Temple University Press, 1990.

Jarvis, P. (ed.). *The Age of Learning: Education and the Knowledge Society.* London: Kogan Page, 2001.

Korten, D. *Getting to the 21st Century: Voluntary Action and the Global Agenda.* West Hartford, Conn.: Kumarian Press, 1990.

Lauzon, A. "Rural Learning." In L. M. English (ed.), *International Encyclopedia of Adult Education.* New York: Palgrave Macmillan, 2005.

Padamsee, D. L., Ewert, D. M., and Deshler, J. D. "Participatory Action Research: A Strategy for Linking Rural Literacy with Community Development, 1996." Retrieved Apr. 12, 2007, from http://www.literacyonline.org/products/ili/pdf/ilprocdp.pdf.

Parks, J., Kennedy, H. L., and Placenti, H. "Adult Literacy in Rural Communities." *Contemporary Education,* 2000, 71(3), 26–29.

Portes, A. "Social Capital: Its Origins and Applications in Modern Sociology." *Annual Review of Sociology,* 1998, 24(1), 1–24.

Putnam, R. D. "The Prosperous Community: Social Capital and Public Life." *American Prospect,* 4(13), 1993, 35–42. Retrieved Apr. 24, 2007, from http://www.epn.org/ prospect/13/13putn.html.

Quigley, B. A. "Literacy." In L. M. English (ed.), *International Encyclopedia of Adult Education.* New York: Palgrave Macmillan, 2005.

Senge, P. *The Fifth Discipline: The Art and Practice of the Learning Organization.* New York: Doubleday, 1990.

Sparks, B., and Peterson, E. "Adult Basic Education and the Crisis of Accountability." In A. L. Wilson and E. R. Hayes (eds.), *Handbook of Adult and Continuing Educat* San Francisco: Jossey-Bass, 2000.

U.S. Census Bureau. "Business and Industry." 2000. Retrieved Apr. 6, 200 http://www.census.gov.

U.S. Department of Agriculture. "Understanding Rural America." 1997. Retri 2006, from http://www.ers.usda.gov/publications/aib710/aib710e.htm.

U.S. Department of Labor. *Current Population Survey.* 2007. Retrieved Ap http://www.bls.gov/cps.

Woolcock, M. "Social Capital and Economic Development: To Synthesis and Policy Framework." *Theory and Society,* 1998, 27

Ziegler, M. F., and Bingman, M. B. "Achieving Adult Education Program Quality: A Review of Systematic Approaches to Program Improvement." In J. Comings, B. Garner, and C. Smith (eds.), *Review of Adult Learning and Literacy: Connecting Research, Policy, and Practice*. Mahwah, N.J.: Erlbaum, 2007.

MARY F. ZIEGLER *is an associate professor in the Educational Psychology and Counseling Department at the University of Tennessee, specializing in adult education.*

DENT C. DAVIS *is dean and vice president for lifelong learning at Columbia Theological Seminary, Decatur, Georgia, where he also teaches courses in leadership and education.*

New Directions for Adult and Continuing Education • DOI: 10.1002/ace

4

This chapter describes a university-based migrant farm-worker outreach and education program in Michigan and the difference it has made in the rural community it serves, as well as in the lives of the university students who have participated in it.

University and Community Collaborations in Migrant ESL

John McLaughlin, Maria Rodriguez, Carolyn Madden

Migrant English as a Second Language (ESL) has been an important form of rural adult education in the United States for decades. It has been recognized as a distinct subfield of both adult education and ESL at least since the mid-1960s, when crucial pieces of federal legislation were passed. Also, activist and professional associations were formed then that engaged in migrant education and/or ESL, for example, Teachers of English to Speakers of Other Languages (TESOL) and the Farm Labor Organizing Committee, both founded in 1966. Migrant ESL is a unique form of adult education in that most programs are carried out at migrant farm camps in rather remote, rural locations through a wide range of organizations and funding streams.

This chapter provides a national and historical overview of rural and migrant ESL. The educational needs of the growing population of seasonal, migrant agricultural workers are discussed and situated in relation to the growth of adult education, literacy education, and ESL as professions in the United States. Then, the majority of this chapter describes and evaluates a migrant farmworker outreach and education program created at the University of Michigan at Ann Arbor and brought to migrant camps in Lenawee County in rural southeastern Michigan. This program, now in its tenth year, has had an important impact on both the university community and the Lenawee County organizations that serve the migrant farmworker populations there. We offer this account as a model for mutually beneficial collaboration among several groups of stakeholders who have provided

NEW DIRECTIONS FOR ADULT AND CONTINUING EDUCATION, no. 117, Spring 2008 © 2008 Wiley Periodicals, Inc.
Published online in Wiley InterScience (www.interscience.wiley.com) • DOI: 10.1002/ace.284

migrant ESL and bilingual health and safety education to adults in rural areas in an era of continuing budget cuts for both adult education and migrant education.

Migrant ESL and Its Relation to Rural Adult Education

Rural ESL began to emerge as a distinct area of ESL in the past decade as migrant agricultural workers settled in rural communities to take year-round jobs. In rural counties around the country, the local Anglo-white population and labor force has decreased due to death, retirement, lower birth rates, and migration to urban and suburban areas, while the Latino and other immigrant workforce moving in has been younger and families have more children. Increasingly there have been more job openings in industries such as nurseries, meatpacking, other forms of food processing, and other service work such as lawn maintenance, as suburban sprawl edges out into formerly rural areas. Berube (2002) cites that 40 percent of limited-English-proficient youth are in rural schools, and the English Language Learner (ELL) population has more than tripled since 1990 from 1.4 million to 4.5 million students in K–12 who are classified as English language learners by the U.S. Department of Education. Demand for training in ESL curriculum and instruction as well as in multicultural education is burgeoning everywhere in rural states and counties across the United States. To address this need, the National Clearinghouse for English Language Acquisition (2006) has recently put out a resource guide for rural education.

The 1960s were a turning point and a point of convergence of developments in adult education, ESL, migrant education, and migrant farmworker activism. Migrant ESL as a distinct subfield of education and ESL arose in the 1960s with the establishment of federally funded migrant education programs and the emergence of ESL as a profession. For example, the U.S. federal government funded Migrant Education Program for school-age migrant farm children began in 1963 (see www.escort.org for further information on the nature of K–12 migrant education). Federal funding for adult education on a national basis began in 1966 (Sticht, 2002). ESL also began to take off as a recognized profession with degree-granting programs (usually a master's degree in TESOL) and various forms of certification and licensure in the 1960s. The end of this decade was also a period of farmworker labor organizing in California and the Midwest, and undoubtedly many paid and volunteer (student) organizers tutored the mostly Spanish-speaking migrant farmworkers while organizing them. While the primarily Spanish-speaking migrant farmworker population continued to grow, the 1970s and 1980s were a period of growth in local adult education programs that served them, including literacy councils and organizations that were usually regional or county based. Other sources of migrant education for adults have included federally funded Migrant Head Start programs for parents and

New Directions for Adult and Continuing Education • DOI: 10.1002/ace

state university extension programs. As with adult education in general, migrant ESL programs have also periodically or frequently experienced fluctuations in federal and state funding due to economic and political vicissitudes. Furthermore, migrant ESL programs are usually seasonal, or run only in the summer in the northern United States, and staff turnover is high as qualified and committed instructors obtain more secure or permanent positions. University service-learning programs are probably the newest arrival on the migrant education scene, and we are aware of only a few other programs around the country hosted in a variety of university schools and departments. For example, the law clinic at the University of Tennessee at Knoxville Law School had a migrant farmworker outreach program, as did the School of Social Work at the University of South Carolina, at least between 2003 and 2005.

Migrant ESL is rooted in both communicative ESL methodology and the popular education principles found in some basic adult literacy classes, often combining Freirean popular education methods, bilingualism, and arts. A published exemplar of this hybrid approach and these methods is documented by Kalmar (2001) based on his experience with Mexican farmworkers in Cobden, Illinois, in the early 1980s. In mainstream ESL, communicative language teaching became the dominant paradigm by the 1970s. It focuses on oral communication as well as basic literacy, incorporating features such as self-contained lessons or modules and materials easily adapted to low-literate, highly mobile populations (see Osterhaudt and Wilkin, 1992, for a good example). Another element that distinguishes this subfield is its setting: migrant ESL is usually carried out at farm camps, out in the open or in makeshift classrooms (barns, trailers, tents) without the usual amenities of a school building. A final distinguishing factor is the range of people who teach migrant ESL, from church volunteers to union and community organizers, from high school and university students to paid community college educators. Church volunteers teaching basic English and Bible stories are among the main providers and sponsors of social services for migrant farmworker families in southeast Michigan, as well as competitors for evening time with other migrant outreach groups.

Migrant Farmworkers in the United States and Their Educational Needs

It is hard to get an accurate count of the 2 to 3 million seasonal and migrant farmworkers in the United States. The U.S. Department of Agriculture estimates that there are at least 1 million migrant male and female adults and 500,000 children and youth who engage in seasonal or temporary agricultural labor, some perhaps having engaged in this work for decades (Thompson and Wiggins, 2002). Due in part to the rural location of employment and residence, these farmworkers have been among the most peripheral and invisible in our society despite their cause-célèbre status among progressive

urban consumers and social activists during periodic boycotts of agricultural and other food products (among them grapes, pickles, Campbell's
Soup, and Taco Bell). Their marginality in our society is aggravated by the
undocumented immigrant status affecting about 50 percent of them. At any
given site, or farm camp, the annual turnover among this population is
extraordinary—about 30 to 40 percent of the workforce. Still, approximately
half of this population has settled into a yearly pattern of migrating from
southern states to the same northern states. Of the 20 million Mexican-born
residents of the United States, perhaps half of them have engaged in seasonal
agricultural labor at some point in their stay, and that form of employment
is an important point of entry in our society. However, given the vast number of migrants and their geographical spread, the current array of adult
education services provided by federal and state governments does not adequately serve this population (Rothenberg, 1998).

Given the hegemonic status of English (proficiency and literacy) as a
condition for obtaining most of the best-paying jobs in the United States,
the educational needs of this population are enormous for those who wish
to enter the mainstream of education and employment. The disrupted
schooling of children and youth perpetuates the migrant farmworker
lifestyle or life cycle. Having a limited range of options for education
before and advancement during employment, migrant farmworkers are
not to be criticized for their choices. It is the persistent poverty and
exploitation of farmworkers in relation to established labor standards gov-
erning employment and working conditions that other industries and
occupations enjoy that should be criticized (see Rothenberg, 1998;
Thompson and Wiggins, 2002). Furthermore, the United States now has
one of the largest Spanish-speaking populations in the Western Hemisphere
but lacks a coherent policy for bilingual education and first-language literacy support, even in most adult education programs. Almost 90 percent
of migrant farmworkers and their families speak Spanish or an indigenous
language of Mexico or Central America. Moreover, although most rural
migrant services are offered bilingually (and for indigenous-language
native speakers, Spanish is already a second language), there are few other
Spanish-language resources in most rural U.S. communities, which creates
other obstacles to participating in adult education in English. Yet migrant
farmworkers are keen on educational opportunities that will lead to more
secure or stable jobs with better pay and working conditions (Arceo,
Kusserow, and Wright, 2002).

In general, most migrant farmworker adults, the majority of whom
have emigrated from Mexico, have limited education. In Mexico, only primary school is compulsory, although not universally enforced, and sec-
ondary school involves fees and long-distance travel for many in rural and
impoverished communities. The average grade level of education of Mexican immigrants is about sixth grade for adults who have emigrated here and
ninth grade for children who have grown up here. Even these average years

of schooling conceal a wide range because many Mexican college graduates have engaged in agricultural labor in the United States, and many Mexican children do not attend or drop out of elementary school due to poverty and migration. The ninth-grade average level of education for children indicates how serious the dropout problem is for migrant students in the United States, and how adult education here is failing to meet their needs as (young) adults, although there are several initiatives for current migrant young adults such as the College Assistance Migrant Program and the High School Equivalency Program (Arceo, Kusserow, and Wright, 2002). Our government and society have an obligation to provide educational opportunities for an otherwise talented and hard-working group of people. In the absence of U.S. efforts, the Mexican government has been providing basic literacy and other educational materials to American school districts and community organizations through the Instituto de los Mexicanos en el Exterior and its network of consulates around the United States (see www.ime.gob.mx for more information in Spanish).

The Migrant ESL and Outreach Program at the University of Michigan, 1996–2006

Readers may be surprised to realize that Michigan has been among the top five of migrant-receiving states and has had between forty-five thousand and ninety thousand migrant farmworkers every summer for decades (probably seventy-five thousand or higher during peak harvest periods). Michigan leads the country in several agricultural crops that must be quickly and delicately harvested by hand, including cherries, pickle cucumbers, and other fruits; vegetables; and flowers. Most of this farmworker population works along Lake Michigan in western Michigan, but there are pockets in central and eastern Michigan that rely heavily on migrant farmworkers (Rochin, Santiago, and Dickey, 1989).

While adult education and ESL services have been developed to serve this population since the 1960s, by the mid-1990s state funding for adult education was drastically reduced by the Republican administration in Michigan. This hurt all adult education and seriously diminished services to the state's migrant population. In an effort to find support for these programs, a migrant educator from the Lenawee County Intermediate School District contacted universities in southeastern Michigan to plead for programmatic and financial support. The English Language Institute (ELI) at the University of Michigan responded with a voluntary effort between 1995 and 1996, which resulted in the recruitment of a linguistics student and an employee interested in Latin American issues. Through the efforts of the ELI's librarian, materials and books were collected for a program in the summer of 1996. With the help of Lenawee County's Community Action Agency and Literacy Council, the program reached six camps in southeast Michigan serving families and single farmworkers. In a year's time, the program was

New Directions for Adult and Continuing Education • DOI: 10.1002/ace

institutionalized, and the College of Literature, Science and Arts and its Office of Multicultural and Academic Initiatives agreed to support the program during the spring and summer semesters for the next four years, from 1997 until 2000.

At the start, the Migrant Outreach Program was facilitated by the ELI and academically supported by the Ginsberg Center for Community Service Learning, where the nationally renowned *Michigan Journal of Community Service Learning* is published. The University of Michigan, one of the nation's leading public research universities, took an early lead in the service-learning movement that grew on American campuses in the 1980s and 1990s. Support has been given to many schools, departments, and institutes on campus to create academic service-learning courses. Academic service-learning courses integrate the service-learning experience as a core content or text of the curricula, while requiring substantial academic preparation before entering the field and continuous oral and written reflection of the experience. The service experience is integral, not extracurricular or even cocurricular. In particular, the migrant ESL program incorporated the expertise of many of the ELI faculty, who provided workshop support for the undergraduate students who participated in learning and teaching ESL and migrant culture for academic credit. Until recently this course was also one of the few that provided a supervised practicum with actual ESL teaching (for credit) for liberal arts undergraduates at the University of Michigan. The program made every attempt to collaborate with other departments for support and expertise, particularly those with migrant outreach programs of their own, such as the Residential College, a select, interdisciplinary liberal arts program; the School of Dentistry; and the School of Medicine's Departments of Psychiatry and Pediatrics.

Besides academic community service-learning, other principles of the Migrant Farmworker Education and Outreach Program have been community collaboration and bilingualism. Fortunately, since the 1970s, Michigan has had a proactive Migrant Services Division in its Department of Human Services, and every region of the state has a Migrant Resource Council. The Southeastern Michigan Migrant Resource Council is one of the largest, and its wide area serves the largest number of migrant farmworkers outside western Michigan. Staff in our program have regularly attended meetings and coordinated with other agencies and organizations through this council to make sure not to interfere with and crowd out other programs at the farm camps and to combine outreach visits as educational for both the ESL learners and the university students (for example, health lessons when the mobile clinics visit the camps).

We have been committed to prolonged engagement and mutual benefit when writing grant proposals and sharing funding, resulting in initiatives such as the Southeastern Michigan Migrant ESL Resource Booklet, a bilingual arts and literacy program for children, and several smaller initiatives in health and arts education. These projects were funded by the University of

New Directions for Adult and Continuing Education • DOI: 10.1002/ace

Michigan Center for Research on Learning and Teaching, the Michigan Campus Compact, the Ginsberg Center for Community Service Learning, and a Michigan Department of Education–administered McKinney-Vento Education of Homeless Children and Youth subgrant. Furthermore, the courses have been cotaught by ESL and Spanish-language educators for the past five years, and the Southeastern Michigan Migrant ESL Resource Booklet is bilingual. The booklet (available at http://www.lsa.umich.edu/eli/instruction/workers/) provides a good sense of what we do in our program.

A Decade of Migrant ESL and Outreach at the University of Michigan

This encounter by liberal arts undergraduates at an elite public university with "rural Michigan/America" has had a positive impact on both students' lives (in terms of their career choices and directions after graduation) and the wider community served by the University of Michigan's Migrant Farmworker Outreach and Education Program (in terms of continuity and collaboration). It is less certain how migrant farmworkers themselves have benefited from our program, as there is only so much that can be done in roughly ten lessons where turnout is affected by the vicissitudes of weather, as well as home and work responsibilities. Nevertheless, this uncertainty is not an argument for discontinuing the program but rather an ongoing inquiry into what would truly serve the educational needs of the migrant farmworker population in our area.

The program has evolved organically with two distinct phases thus far, and perhaps entering a third as faculty coordinators turn over every five years or so. It is a physically and emotionally intense experience for both university students and instructors, one that requires working evenings and getting home late, after 11:00 P.M. Perhaps one interesting way to look at how the program has changed over time is to see how the migrant farmworkers have been served.

Originally there were two separate programs: ESL and Spanish Outreach. The ESL program worked by primarily teaching English to adult men. In the initial stages, visits were made to the various camps in order to solicit support from the farm owners and then to canvass workers and their families, gathering commitments from the workers to attend classes. While migrant workers are legally eligible to have visitors at their housing site, the situation in migrant camps is a particularly sensitive one, with many farm owners cautious about publicizing the housing and living conditions of migrant workers. The outreach program in Spanish also visited the same camps, but its focus was to provide information to the migrant population in their native language, ensuring that the families understood and were able to participate in the discussions. This course tended to work with both adults and children, as it was necessary to devise activities to keep the children occupied while the students provided presentations on health issues and conducted pesticide safety trainings with adults or served as translators for medical clinics.

Due to the logistics of funding, staffing, and coordination, as well as a renewed commitment to bilingualism as a critical approach to ESL, those two programs were combined in 2002. The new combined course no longer provided health information, but the students continued to be trained in Spanish to present pesticide safety issues and provide basic medical translation. We realized that to involve women in the ESL program, we needed to offer separate classes from the men as well as to teach the children simultaneously, which our combined program started doing fully by 2004. In this way, women were freed from familial responsibilities and were able to focus on their lessons, and the teaching interns were able to design lesson plans that reflected women's and men's diverging needs and interests as to language use. The children's classes have fully taken root in the past three years, although adult women's classes have been harder to sustain consistently at all three camps. A next direction would be to incorporate more vocational or career-oriented lessons in the program. Automotive maintenance is very popular, but few university students appear to have much skill (or vocabulary) in this area.

Over the years, the migrant farmworkers have come to expect our program at the three main camps in Lenawee County. In addition, the coordination of the wide array of services we provide or tie in with has been a primary strength. The success of the summer program has been measured along many variables. The number of migrant students attending the evening classes, after a long day picking fruits or vegetables, was a significant marker for the individual intern teacher's feeling of success (depending on the year and the camp, overall turnout varies from ten to twenty-five students every visit). Migrants themselves voiced how much they valued the intern's work by offering to pay for evening ESL classes after the official academic course was completed. In fact, many undergraduates have continued teaching as volunteers with "their students" beyond the academic semester.

For the ELI and the university, the integration of experience with academic reflection for the student interns was another measure of success. The students' reflection papers were a significant testimony to the influence of the experience on their lives and academic careers. We require a research paper in the spring on an issue affecting migrant farmworkers in the United States, but in the summer term, many students opt to do a creative art project with a shorter essay at the end of the course because words alone cannot capture or convey their experience. One undergraduate in the College of Literature, Science and Arts, who was determined to go to law school, delayed the professional school experience for a year to volunteer to teach ESL abroad. Others expressed an increased awareness and a deeper understanding of injustices and poverty and their many causes here at home. Still others looked for more global venues, such as the Peace Corps, in which to continue their experience and education. Several students have created campus and community organizations to serve Spanish-speaking migrant and immigrant workers in the area. From creating an arts program to an academic tutoring program, to a workers' center with ESL programs run jointly with a church, our students have done extraordinary things with their experience. In addition, the local migrant advocacy community and the farmworkers themselves enjoy their interaction and connection with our university program. Nevertheless, it is heartbreaking to leave the camps for the last time every August, knowing we have made at most a small difference in the lives and education of the farmworkers and children themselves.

Our effect on the migrants' language development has always been less satisfying. In spite of an enormous effort and commitment by staff and faculty, the interns are given a short course in teaching ESL and asked to teach in very difficult and challenging situations. The ELI and Linguistics Department sponsored a research project to evaluate and assess the value of the program on the language of the migrants. While it was obvious that within this short period of time language was not much improved, the impact of the connections and the commitment served to increase the farm growers' appreciation for the university's interest and presence. It also created expectations on the part of the migrants that there was support from outside the farming community for their plight and their well-being. What gets developed is probably the confidence that comes from sympathetic, at times bilingual, interactions with diverse Americans.

A tacit attraction of the migrant outreach program for university students and faculty is the possibility to enter a different world of rural farm communities in Michigan that is both a culture shock and a pleasure (perhaps nostalgia for America's agricultural past?). There is a sense of traveling back in time while driving along Highway 12, the old stagecoach road between Detroit and Chicago, with its many farms and several abandoned farmhouses and collapsed barns along the way. Another shock on reentry into downtown Ann Arbor as the vans unload at night is that such large concentrations of cultural and linguistic others exist in that world that we are unaware of as we buy the food they harvest. This brief summer experience connects us with the rural, agricultural roots that most of us share at some point in our family trees. The bonds we form among program participants, including the migrant farmworkers, though brief, are intense and profound.

References

Arceo, R., Kusserow, J., and Wright, A. "Understanding the Challenges and Potential of Migrant Students." In C. Thompson Jr. and M. Wiggins (eds.), *The Human Cost of Food*. Austin: University of Texas Press, 2002.

Berube, B. "Three Rs for ESL Instruction in U.S. Rural Schools: A Test of Commitment." *TESOL Matters*, 2002, 12(4).Retrieved June 23, 2007, from http://www.tesol.org/s_tesol/sec_document.

Kalmar, T. M. *Illegal Alphabets and Adult Biliteracy: Latino Migrants Crossing the Linguistic Border*. Mahwah, N.J.: Erlbaum, 2001.

National Clearinghouse for English Language Acquisition. "Rural Education." 2006. Retrieved June 23, 2007, from http://www.ncela.gwu.edu/resbout/rural/index.html.

Osterhaudt, B., and Wilkin, B. "The Glide, the Sting, the Rescue: ESL Instruction for Migrant Farmworkers." *TESOL Journal*, 1992, 2(1), 17–21.

Rochin, R. I., Santiago, A. M., and Dickey, K. S. *Migrant and Seasonal Workers in Michigan's Agriculture: A Study of Their Contributions, Characteristics, Needs and Services.* East Lansing: Julian Samora Research Institute, Michigan State University, 1989.

Rothenberg, D. *With These Hands: The Hidden World of Migrant Farmworkers Today.* Berkeley: University of California Press, 1998.

Sticht, T. G. "The Rise of the Adult Education and Literacy System in the United States, 1600–2000." 2002. Retrieved Apr. 30, 2007, from www.ncsall.net/?id=576.

Thompson, C. D., and Wiggins, M. F. *The Human Cost of Food: Farmworkers' Lives, Labor and Advocacy.* Austin: University of Texas Press, 2002.

JOHN MCLAUGHLIN *is an educational specialist in the Consolidated Federal Program Support Division of the Minnesota Department of Education and was the coordinator of the University of Michigan's Migrant Farmworker Outreach and Education Program from 2002 to 2006.*

MARIA RODRIGUEZ *is a lecturer in Spanish in the Residential College and coordinator of the Migrant Farmworker Outreach and Education Program at the University of Michigan, Ann Arbor.*

CAROLYN MADDEN *is a senior lecturer and associate director for curriculum and instruction at the University of Michigan English Language Institute. She founded the English Language Institute's Migrant Worker Program in 1996.*

New Directions for Adult and Continuing Education • DOI: 10.1002/ace

5

Meeting the learning needs of older adults in rural areas is a critical and growing concern for adult and continuing education. This chapter addresses learning in a rural context for older adults.

Rural Education for Older Adults

Vivian W. Mott

The population of the United States is aging dramatically. Of the more than 300 million people in the United States, more than 25 percent of those are beyond the age of 55, and that number continues to swell. The mean age in 2005 was 36.2, for instance, and is projected to increase at an average of six months annually through 2030 (U.S. Census, 2004). At the time of the 2000 census, approximately 56 million people in the United States were over the age of 55, and more than 12 million of these individuals lived in rural, non-metropolitan areas (U.S. Census, 2004). Our current seniors, and those who continue to age behind them, are among the best educated our society has ever seen. The 2000 census revealed that while an approximate 14 million people beyond the age of 55 had less than a high school diploma, 20 million were high school graduates, and more than 22 million had some college—an undergraduate or advanced college degree (U.S. Census, 2004). Some of the changes occurring in rural populations are the result of in-migration: many among those relocating are retirees with higher levels of education and consequently greater interest and needs in continuing education. This higher level of educational attainment, coupled with the ever increasing complexity of our society, increased dependency on constantly changing technology, and quickened knowledge obsolescence, suggests that rural older adults have complex, dynamic, and varied learning needs. When one considers these complex and dynamic factors, the issue of providing for the learning needs of vast numbers of older adults living in rural, non-metropolitan areas becomes especially critical to the adult and continuing educators and institutions that serve them.

NEW DIRECTIONS FOR ADULT AND CONTINUING EDUCATION, no. 117, Spring 2008 © 2008 Wiley Periodicals, Inc.
Published online in Wiley InterScience (www.interscience.wiley.com) • DOI: 10.1002/ace.285

Older Adult Learning in a Rural Context

In order to explore the learning needs of older rural adults, it is necessary to first examine several constructs. These include the definitions of *rural*, the issues of the learners' ages, and the various structures and purposes their learning takes. While all of these constructs can be widely debated, this section provides the boundaries and rationales for these concepts on which points in the chapter are based.

The Rural Older Adult. According to the U.S. Census of 2000, an estimated 12 million older adults live in what are classified as rural areas of the nation (U.S. Census, 2004). The term *rural*, however commonly used in conversation and descriptions of places and people, is more difficult to define precisely. *Rural* is officially considered to be "any unincorporated place . . . with fewer than 2,500 inhabitants" (U.S. Department of Agriculture, 2007), to include farms, towns, and small cities located outside urban or metropolitan areas. More important to any working definition of *rurality*, however, might be the need to challenge our nostalgic, idealized conceptions of *rural*. Images of seniors puttering in gardens or workshops, picturesque farms on quiet country roads, and quaint small-town libraries and quilting bees are perhaps an accurate portrayal of the rural landscape and its inhabitants, but they are insufficient.

Another concept important to explore, *older adults*, is equally difficult to pin down. Bjorklund and Bee (2007) define three classifications of older adults in terms of their ages. The young-old are those between the ages of sixty-five and seventy-five, middle-old adults are those seventy-five to eighty-five years old, and the oldest-old are those beyond the age of eighty-five. Because many institutions, organizations, and social policies define older adults as persons beyond the age of fifty-five, however, this discussion will be based on the broader age range of fifty-five and beyond. This age range also includes the significant, and still youthful if aging baby boomers, whose higher educational attainment, continuing education needs for career and "rewiring" for second careers, and pure love for learning further define the complex and dynamic rural context.

Inherent in this depiction of rural older adults and their potential learning needs are additional considerations of sparse population, isolation from social interaction and support networks, lack of infrastructure and services, and difficulty in transportation; all of these can influence both learning interests and needs, as well as the ability to engage in learning opportunities. These issues serve as both motivations and potential barriers for learning in later years; as such, seniors' rural lifestyle, broad range of learning and social interests, and practical needs related to quality of life all provide an incredible array of learning possibilities.

The Learning Context. Learning throughout life can occur in a number of ways. One of the more common classifications of learning contexts (an adaptation of an earlier categorization) is presented by Merriam, Caffarella,

New Directions for Adult and Continuing Education • DOI: 10.1002/ace

and Baumgartner (2007), who categorize learning as formal, informal, or nonformal. They suggest that much of the adult and continuing learning that immediately comes to mind is formal, occurring in institutional environments, usually requiring payment of fees or tuition, and "formally recognized with grades, diplomas, or certificates" (p. 29). Much of the learning provided for rural older adults, however, is nonformal or informal and characterized as "local and community-based, such as those programs offered by museums, libraries, service clubs, religious and civic organizations" (p. 30) or undertaken by the learners themselves or in small community groups. Health education, a topic of interest and importance in most rural communities, provides an excellent example of content pursued in each of these three forms of formal, nonformal, and informal learning. An older adult learner could formally pursue a degree or certificate as a nursing assistant, for example, either to return to the workplace after retirement or to serve in a volunteer capacity in a small rural clinic. Another older rural resident, as a result of a recent diagnosis of some medical condition, might enroll in a nonformal health management or nutrition class at the local community college or provided by a health care provider or pharmaceutical firm. Examples of informal health education could be conversations that take place among friends or families as medical conditions are discussed, information gained from medication brochures or waiting room magazines, or by viewing a television program.

The purposes for which older adults pursue learning are essential for educators and program planners for rural older adults to consider as well. Houle's prominent typology of learning orientations, known widely as Houle's typology (1988), describes learners as goal oriented, learning oriented, or activity oriented. In this typology, goal-oriented learners are motivated by an objective or purpose that may be achieved through a learning experience. Examples for older rural learners might include learning about the Internet or e-mail in order to stay in contact with family members who live at a distance or the pursuit of a nutritional cooking class to combat a health issue. Learning-oriented individuals pursue learning for the sake of learning alone; they represent the classic image of a lifelong learner and the nineteenth-century ideal of liberal arts education. Older learners in this category could be interested in organic gardening, spirituality, philosophy, or classics in American literature solely for the joy of learning. Activity orientation is often thought to be the primary motivation for many older learners, since the focus of activity-oriented learning is the activity or social interaction itself. The same topics already noted could be pursued for the activities associated with them; computer training, a cooking or gardening class, or a book club might be more about coming together with friends or neighbors than focused on the learning that happens incidentally through the gathering.

Jarvis (1983, 2006) also theorized that learning may be less about the articulated motivations of adults, but instead a reflection of sociocultural pressures and the "dynamic tension that exists between the learner" (1983, p. 67) and the transitions in one's life at any given time. Retired individuals may discover, for instance, the need for more education or training to return to paid employment, the desire to learn more about a new medical diagnosis and available treatment, or the pursuit of a new hobby or avocation, all as a result of their life transitions.

Two models of aging and retirement help explain and integrate Houle's learning orientations and Jarvis's description of the influence of dynamic tension on learning pursuits. According to major scholars in gerontology (see, for instance, Atchley 1972, 1989; Butler and Gleason, 1985; and Erikson, Erikson, and Kivnick, 1986), activity theory and continuity theory are two models of normal aging. Activity theory suggests that older adults age more successfully when they keep busy and engage fully in activities they enjoy. Activity-oriented older adults who can take advantage of learning pursuits, then, are conceivably happier and enjoy a greater degree of physical and mental health. Continuity theory was proposed by Atchley (1972) as a "grand adaptive theory" to explain the continuation of social behaviors into later life. The simple continuation of routine, behaviors, and lifestyle helps to maintain a higher quality of life, physical health, and mental rigor. Pursuit of learning opportunities, often prompted by life transitions (dynamic tensions), provides the means of continuity for many older rural adults.

These two models of older adults' motivations for learning are instrumental in facilitating the effective planning, design, and delivery of programs in rural communities. By understanding seniors' motivations and purposes for their learning, adult and continuing educators will be able to provide more successful learning opportunities for this unique group.

The Structure of Rural Older Learning Opportunities

Planning learning opportunities for rural older learners involves consideration of which partners and collaborators might best provide the education, attention to the complex and dynamic elements of effective program planning, and concern for the actual instruction and learning interaction.

Partners and Collaborators. The providers of learning opportunities for rural older adults are as varied as the opportunities themselves. Because of the rural context of learners' daily lives, partners and collaborators may appear somewhat limited but are critical to the success of programs. Providers include a wide variety of associations, institutions, and organizations: religious institutions; local school systems; university extension services; farm organizations such as the Grange; women's clubs and book discussion groups; museums and libraries; health care providers; service clubs such as Ruritan, Rotary, or Optimists; social service agencies; 4H and recreation centers; local business and industries; government agencies; and grassroots community organizations. Providers will find it critical to gather input from community members and the learners themselves in order to ensure local buy-in and support. Providers who are invested in and known by the community are more successful. Partners and collaborators who are seen as part of the community, sensitive to the needs and diversity of the older adults, and knowledgeable of the resources and possible constraints of the rural community are in a better position to maximize educational offerings for older learners.

Program Planning and Instructional Materials. There is a wealth of program planning models for adult and continuing education. According to Caffarella (2002), program planning models "come in all shapes and sizes . . . [and] may be simplistic in their orientation . . . or very complex" p. 15). Whether linear, nonsequential, reiterative, or interactive, program planning consists of a series of steps necessary to conceive of a program idea, bring the program to fruition, and evaluate the outcomes and possible future of the program. Caffarella's interactive model of program planning, one of the more comprehensive of such models, outlines twelve steps, which include the determination of context and program ideas, design and development of instruction, attention to budget and marketing, facilities coordination, and coalition building and evaluation.

Where program planning for rural older adults is concerned, some of the steps are more crucial than others. Because of the potential impact of age-related changes concerning vision, hearing, and mobility, attention to accessibility, transportation, appropriate space, furniture, and equipment is important. Among the more critical steps in the provision of learning for older adults in any context is attention to the design and development of materials and the actual instruction itself. Because of the age-related issues, care must be taken in the development of materials, the arrangement of the learning space in terms of lighting and sound, use of computer and audio-visual equipment, and the activities themselves.

Active Learner-Centered Instruction. Any learning opportunity is a function of the interaction of the learner, instructor or facilitator, content, and environment or context. And as with all other adult learning, active, learner-centered instruction is dependent largely on the appropriate choice of instructional strategies by an instructor or facilitator who is committed to active, engaged, interactive learning. Regardless of the instructional strategies chosen, older rural adult learners in particular respond to well-delivered, relevant content, engagement and dialogue, and the inclusion of experiential activities. They appreciate time to share their experiences, their lifelong store of wisdom, and their practical expertise. Instructional strategies that incorporate these interactive elements not only ensure a learner orientation to the instruction but help make critical cognitive connections that support active learning and retention.

New Directions for Adult and Continuing Education • DOI: 10.1002/ace

Case Studies

Actual and hypothetical case studies often promote a better understanding of models and theories as well as effective practices that can derive from such models by portraying people, their circumstances, goals, and challenges. The case studies that follow represent three very different groups of rural, older learners in pursuit of education for a variety of purposes: learning for self-sufficiency, social action, and leisure or self-improvement.

Learning for Economic Self-Sufficiency. Among the more crucial learning motivations in any context is learning for self-sufficiency. Many research studies indicate that the purpose of most adult and continuing learning is self-sufficiency: learning to secure a job and income, advancing one's career, or otherwise being able to provide for oneself and family (see, for example, Aslanian, 2001; Valentine, 1997). This holds no less true for older adults in rural areas, as demonstrated by this case study.

In an isolated rural community in the Appalachians, approximately 650 residents lived in abject poverty. The average family income was less than $8,000 annually, compared to poverty guidelines for 2001 in the continental United States of $8,500 for one person, $11,600 for two, and $17,600 for a family of four (U.S. Department of Health and Human Services, 2005). The typical extended household included several children, usually a single parent, and often two or more older family members: aunts, uncles, cousins, grandparents, and even great-grandparents. More than fifty older adults, ages 56 to 102, lived alone in the community. Approximately 20 percent of the adults worked in one of three commercial establishments in their small crossroads community or in one of four neighboring towns within a radius of thirty-five to fifty miles. The community itself was home to a small market, gas station, and discount store, as well as a health clinic (staffed only one or two days a week), two churches, and a community center that housed a limited library, a pool table, and pinball machines that no longer functioned.

The small community faced a variety of citizen needs. With help from their county extension agent, the state agencies on aging and social services, and a retired teacher-librarian, the seniors in the community set out to provide for their own needs and those of their community. A community needs assessment revealed the most pressing and consistent needs to be home health care, assistance with activities of daily living (ADLs), and child care and elder care services. Program planning and curriculum development were provided by the retired teacher and county extension agent. Financial support for learning materials and supplies came from a neighboring church and Rotary club, and the largely vacant community center became a vibrant adult learning center. The community's new Senior Action Group (SAG) was born.

Within three months of the first meeting of SAG, the older adults in the community had opened a small child care facility that enabled fifteen fathers and mothers to work in neighboring towns, provided continuing medical education to two senior nursing assistants who staffed the small clinic and provided some home health care and ADL services, and supported a three-generation team of women in the opening of their own elder care facility. Future classes were being planned for a peer hospice and grief support program, volunteer tax preparation, and financial counseling. Through SAG and their own determination and self-directed learning, these older learners in rural Appalachia regenerated their community, provided greatly needed services, and enhanced their self-sufficiency and quality of life.

Learning for Social Action. In an isolated rural community in the south-central United States, learning for an engaged group of older adults took the form of social action. This case study describes a very small community with fewer than eighty families, the majority of whom were African American and over the age of fifty. The majority of the residents were retired or disabled, and most tended small garden plots adjacent to their homes. The few residents who still worked did so in neighboring towns twenty-five to thirty miles away. The community was literally a dying crossroads with a general store on one corner and a vacant gas station and kudzu-covered storefront on two others. The fourth corner stood overgrown as a railroad easement and right-of-way. A former school housed a small volunteer health clinic that was staffed only occasionally, and another building stood empty except for the wind and wildlife that crept in unnoticed. There were three churches in the community, all within walking distance of the majority of homes. Some of the residents lived without indoor plumbing, and many had no telephones or television. Surrounding the simple, small frame homes were thousands of acres of timber, tobacco, soybeans, and peanuts, which added to the idyllic agrarian image of the community.

When the long-standing crop cycle of planting and harvesting was interrupted one year, one of the older residents noticed and wondered why the fields lay fallow—fields previously aggressively managed by absentee corporate landowners. Conversations followed in the general store, before and after church services, and along the road as the townspeople went about their daily affairs. When another resident noticed a small rezoning sign on the fence surrounding one large field, they sought the assistance of distant children and grandchildren, local politicians, and a nearby junior college to investigate the drastic changes about to be imposed on their way of life.

Their investigation to determine the names, organizational structure, and location of the absentee landowners included an organized and persistent letter-writing and telephone campaign. The residents pooled their knowledge, experience, and resources in order to travel en masse, first to the county seat and then to the state capitol, to gather the information needed concerning pending land use changes. As a result, the townspeople learned that a huge pork producer was planning two large hog farms: farms that would virtually enclose their small community and compromise their air and water quality.

New Directions for Adult and Continuing Education • DOI: 10.1002/ace

As the residents began to take action to save their community, they had lots to learn. Fewer than a dozen of the residents had attended college, and many had not finished high school; now their self-directed learning in service of their investigation included computer instruction, Internet-based exploration, and lessons in grant writing. Most of the townspeople had previously gone for weeks without seeing anyone they had not known for most of their lives; they were now interacting almost daily with lawyers, business leaders, agricultural and environmental experts, and politicians. Many of them had never traveled out of their county, yet their social action took them ultimately to the halls of Congress to lobby with legislators to save their community.

The outcome is uncertain for this small, crossroads community of rural elderly. They were successful in saving one large tract of adjoining land, securing the land through a conservancy as a natural wildlife preserve; however, thousands of acres remain at risk. Some of the residents remain active in their self-initiated social action to save their homes, health, and quiet quality of life. All of them are more engaged in the community and with their own self-directed learning, health, and daily activities.

Learning for Leisure. In this final case study, the focus turns to learning for leisure and self-improvement. This example is drawn from a small community of vibrant older learners in a small town in the rural western United States—a haven for retired teachers, physicians, businessmen and businesswomen, military personnel, and others who enjoy the climate, cultural diversity, and natural environment. The residents included approximately three hundred individuals, ages fifty-six to ninety-two, and representing significant racial/ethnic diversity. Most were married, but there were also more than fifty single individuals. The collective health of the residents was excellent, and most enjoyed some degree of financial comfort in their retirement. The shared persona and general consensus of the group was that the liberation of retirement should also provide a high degree of social interaction, continued formal and nonformal learning, and recreational and intellectual pursuits. Thus, the group sought ways to bring those pursuits to their remote community.

This eclectic rural community grew out of the single purchase of a small ranch by a group of friends and business colleagues. The community included several thousand acres of rugged open terrain, and the renovated cabins and new homes were miles apart from one another. What had once been a lodge near the center of the original ranch was collaboratively renovated to become a combined conference center, music hall, and recreation center. The center facility was soon joined by stables, a swimming pool, tennis courts, an eighteen-hole golf course, and marked hiking trails. The residents formed an advisory board to assist in the administration and management of the education and recreation centers in their community. Several of the residents had taken part in Elderhostel or Learning in Retirement sessions prior to relocating to the desert; the board adopted the model of

liberal arts and adventure-based lifelong learning as a hallmark of their community. An education director was hired, and the program planning for their
leisure learning began in earnest.

The needs and interest assessment revealed not only the expected wide
range of interests, but also suggested a vast degree of expertise and instructional talent among the residents. Thus, much of the instruction was conducted by the residents themselves. When the expertise for a desired topic
was not available among them, one of the residents frequently took the initiative to pursue the necessary knowledge to be passed on to others. On
occasion, guest instructors were contracted and given accommodations in
the center for the duration of the class. Residents were levied a designated
amount each year to fund the administration and overhead of the centers,
and then paid fees for the classes they took. Among the education classes
provided were golf, swimming, equestrian training, and tennis lessons, as
well as classes in desert flora and fauna, Native American history, and geol-
ogy. There were language and music classes, art and pottery instruction, and
culinary and nutrition classes.

Summary. These three case studies present vastly different populations
of rural, older learners, but all in pursuit of education for a variety of purposes. The three represent learning for self-sufficiency, social action, and
leisure and self-improvement. The older learners all lived in rural areas of
the United States, but in very different communities; they represented the
diversity that exists among all older adults regarding age, ethnicity, and education and also in terms of interests, motivations, and potential barriers.
Their learning orientations, according to Houle (1988), were goal oriented
in the Appalachian and African American communities and activity
and learning oriented for the western retirees. The dynamic tension suggested by Jarvis (1983) differed for each group as well. One group sought
to provide more completely for themselves and others in poverty-stricken
Appalachia; another learned to engage in social action to preserve the quality of their community and daily life; and another sought to learn something
new while maintaining their active, engaged lifestyle. The instructional and
organizational assistance and learning that supported each group of older
rural learners were more successful with attention given to context, motivations, and characteristics of the learners in each community context.

Implications for Theory and Practice

There are significant implications for both theory and practice in adult and
continuing education. The case studies point to the necessity of understanding the lives and context of older learners in rural areas. Fundamental
knowledge in gerontology, adult development, life transitions, program
planning, and effective teaching are critical to the success of rural educational
programming for older adults. Program planning and implementation of
learning opportunities for older rural adults require an understanding of the

life contexts, interests and needs, and characteristics of the learners. It is important to consider factors such as transportation, cost, age, health, and technological capability, while not assuming these influences to be barriers to participation and success.

Finally, these case studies reinforce many of the tenets of adult and continuing education and suggest critical directions for those who work in rural education or with older learners. Freire's pedagogy and praxis suggest that the best education regardless of age is dialogic, participatory, and situated in the lived experiences of the learners; it embraces conscientization (the developing of consciousness to transform one's reality) and enhances both community and social capital (Freire, 1972, 1995). A final lesson learned should be that education is never value free—that one's ethics and value system should be transparent and used to ground practice. Given the common strong sense of ethics of older rural adults, as well as the great promise held in learning opportunities provided them, adult and continuing educators have the enviable challenge of meeting the learning needs of rural older adults while facilitating their successful aging and continued quality of life.

References

Aslanian, C. B. *Adult Students Today.* New York: College Board, 2001.

Atchley, R. C. *The Social Forces in Later Life: An Introduction to Social Gerontology.* Belmont, Calif.: Wadsworth, 1972.

Atchley, R. C. "A Continuity Theory of Normal Aging." *Gerontologist,* 1989, 29(2), 183–190.

Bjorklund, B. R., and Bee, H. L. *The Journey of Adulthood.* (6th ed.) Upper Saddle River, N.J.: Prentice Hall, 2007.

Butler, R., and Gleason, H. (eds.). *Productive Aging: Enhancing Vitality in Later Life.* New York: Springer, 1985.

Caffarella, R. S. *Planning Programs for Adult Learners.* (2nd ed.) San Francisco: Jossey-Bass, 2002.

Erikson, J. M., Erikson, E. H., and Kivnick, H. *Vital Involvement in Old Age.* New York: Norton, 1986.

Freire, P. *Pedagogy of the Oppressed.* New York: Continuum, 1995.

Freire, P. *Pedagogy of Hope. Reliving Pedagogy of the Oppressed.* New York: Continuum, 1995.

Houle, C. O. *The Inquiring Mind.* (2nd ed.) Norman: Oklahoma Research Center for Continuing Professional and Higher Education, 1988. (Original work published in 1961)

Jarvis, P. *Adult and Continuing Education: Theory and Practice.* London: Croom Helm, 1983.

Jarvis, P. *Towards a Comprehensive Theory of Human Learning.* London: Routledge/Falmer Press, 2006.

Merriam, S. B., Caffarella, R. S., and Baumgartner, L. M. *Learning in Adulthood.* (3rd ed.) San Francisco: Jossey-Bass, 2007.

U.S. Census Bureau. "Census 2000: Population and Household Economics Topics." 2004. Retrieved Apr. 10, 2007, from http://www.census.gov/population/socdemo/age/ppl-147/tab21.txt.

U.S. Department of Agriculture. Economic Research Service. "Measuring Rurality: What Is Rural?" 2007. Retrieved Apr. 10, 2007, from http://www.ers.usda.gov/Briefing/Rurality/WhatisRural/.

U.S. Department of Health and Human Services. "The 2001 HHS U.S. Poverty Guide-lines. One Version of the [U.S.] Federal Poverty Measure." 2005. Retrieved Apr. 20, 2007, from http://aspe.hhs.gov/poverty/01poverty.htm.

Valentine, T. "United States of America: The Current Predominance of Learning for the Job." In P. Belander and S. Valdivielso (eds.), *The Emergence of Learning Societies: Who Participates in Adult Learning?* New York: Elsevier, 1997.

VIVIAN W. MOTT *is professor and chair of the Department of Counselor and Adult Education in the College of Education at East Carolina University, Greenville.*

New Directions for Adult and Continuing Education • DOI: 10.1002/ace

6

Interviews with bush Alaskan educators offer a close-up perspective of the challenges surrounding the adoption of information, communication, and educational technologies in rural areas.

Information, Communication, and Educational Technologies in Rural Alaska

G. Andrew Page, Melissa Hill

Information, communication, and educational technologies hold promise to connect geographically isolated rural communities, offering adults greater access to educational, financial, and numerous other resources (Dorr and Besser, 2002; Lenhart and others, 2003; Page, 2004; Pittman, 2003; Stark, 2002). The Internet and computer-based network technologies are often seen as remedies for communities in economic decline, but they also have the potential to divide (Postman, 1993). When the tool of technology is not effectively introduced and proper training not offered, potential exists to widen the schism (Schiller, 1996) between the coexisting and competing social systems of indigenous people and non-Natives (Prakash and Esteva, 2005; Wimburg and others, 2003). This chapter provides insight into the issues surrounding the diffusion of information and communication technologies into rural Alaskan communities. A contemporary analysis of the impediments that challenge rural Alaskans and the implications of change from the adoption of innovations is provided.

Background

The world has become increasingly dependent on computer technologies in many aspects of daily life, from business to entertainment to education. In the urban environment, many are acclimated to the rich technological world of advanced multimedia, and technological communication continues to

NEW DIRECTIONS FOR ADULT AND CONTINUING EDUCATION, no. 117, Spring 2008 © 2008 Wiley Periodicals, Inc.
Published online in Wiley InterScience (www.interscience.wiley.com) • DOI: 10.1002/ace.286

transform modern culture in such a way that interaction with technology occurs without conscious effort. In 1993, President Bill Clinton highlighted the changing role of technology in the global economy as follows: "Most important of all, information has become global and has become king of the global economy. In earlier history, wealth was measured in land, gold, in oil, in machines. Today, the principal measure of our wealth is information: its quality, its quantity, and the speed with which we acquire it and adapt to it" (cited in Schiller, 1996, p. 105).

Technology is continually changing the way we learn, work, and live (Wilson, Notar, and Yunker, 2003). While information has the potential to transcend the bounds of time, place, and space, in rural areas disparity exists regarding the diffusion of information and communication technologies. A powerful and critical view of technology, digital information, and cyberspace directed toward those outsiders who support the diffusion of technology is offered by Prakash and Esteva (2005): "We know that we do not know how to bring you along to savor the flavors of our vernacular worlds. We know that the lived pluriverse—of spoken vernacular tongues, of feasts and flavors, of suffering and celebration—cannot be reduced to information. It is too rich, alive, and vibrant to be keyed into the memory bits and bytes that run the educational industry today" (p. 30).

Research by Lenhart and others (2003) found that in rural America, 31 percent of rural African Americans use the Internet compared with 44 percent of rural whites. Again, the correlation between poverty or income and technological availability surfaces as 70 percent of rural African Americans live in households with incomes of less than thirty thousand dollars a year; in comparison, only 44 percent of rural whites have incomes that are less than thirty thousand dollars. Swain and Pearson (2003) look at the significant differences in equity and access to technology in the United States based on demographic categories such as income, race, gender, location, and education. The many digital divides found in this research are systemic in rural areas. "This [disparity] is a significant problem that reaches across all economic levels, but is especially serious at schools with lower economic status" (p. 330). The disparity is in the equity of access to information. Information is knowledge, and in an increasingly global culture, one has to ask, Shouldn't everyone have access to technology? Or will technology be the impetus to reinforce the class system? At the same time, do individuals who identify themselves as rural promote the class system? What role does technology play in rural community, and who defines that role? These challenges raise questions of access to information through technology and issues of equity.

The research reveals that the issue of the diffusion of technology into rural areas is complex. Themes of change, identity, empowerment, and transformation emerge from it. As part of her work on empowering communities, Pittman (2003) found that learners can benefit from "strategic uses of technology" (p. 53). She states: "Adults in homes, schools, and community centers need to embrace, not fear, technology and believe in its transformative power; they must develop new capacities to embed technology in all of their work. We owe learners many and varied ways to experience technology's value in the learning process and use it to take charge of their own learning" (p. 53).

How are individuals in rural areas adapting to this fast-paced global change brought about by the diffusion of information and communication technologies? Based on our own experience, we have found that some rural communities are reticent to embrace new technologies; many residents of rural communities fear that members of the next generation will become so dependent on information technology that they will lose their innate ability to function in their pragmatic sensible world, which relies more on intuition than information. Consider this example: a resident of a remote village in rural Alaska is better off learning how to navigate the land by observation, human senses, and reading the stars, rather than using an electronic device such as a global positioning satellite navigation system.

The Culture Factor

Fear exists that when technological information fails, there will be no intuition to draw on, and it is that very intuition that has created identity in generation after generation. In addressing the postcolonial administration of education in rural Alaska, Deniro (2004) found that although the curriculum was "well meaning," it was "often culturally insensitive" (p. 401) and was implemented with little regard for indigenous values. It has been widely documented that culture plays an important role in how innovations such as the use of computer technologies are adopted (Albirini, 2006; Williams-Green, Holmes, and Sherman, 1997; Straub, Keil, and Brenner, 1997). Haynes Writer (Wimburg and others, 2003) provides an insightful response to how indigenous people such as Alaska Natives are "operating within an economic and cultural schism" with regard to technology and suggests that native people "must be creative in our use of technology so we are in control of it rather than having it control us" (p. 34).

Nonetheless, the world is changing, and as technology becomes more integrated as a necessity for daily life, access to technology will become as important as access to education. Stark (2002) provides an assessment of what needs to be accomplished in rural areas:

> If information technology is to create jobs and generate income [through] rural communications, rural people must have ready access to computers and the Internet; yet large numbers of citizens still do not. In fact, the individuals who would most benefit from distance learning, technology skill development, and other online tools are least likely to have computers and the Internet available at home or work, and to know how to employ information technology effectively [p. 25].

New Directions for Adult and Continuing Education • DOI: 10.1002/ace

Digital empowerment is critical to the economic and social livelihood of these rural communities. Norris (2001) writes about a mobilization of marginalized groups and how individuals can be empowered through the Internet and the many opportunities associated with information literacy. Yet there is a delicate balance that must be achieved between the simultaneous desire to change and sustain. The next section provides the perspective of three rural Alaskan educators on the issues they face with technology in their practice.

Technology and Rural Alaska

The context for rural Alaska is different from rural communities in the Lower Forty-Eight. Many of the villages or bush hubs are located off the road system, accessible only by air, and in some cases only by small bush airplanes. In some remote communities, mail and other freight are delivered only weekly. In winter, rivers freeze and become highways that snow machines, trucks, and dog teams travel across. The communities off the road system are predominantly populated by Alaskan Natives indigenous to the region, who still speak their native language. They struggle to maintain their cultural heritage and values. Many Alaska Natives still practice a subsistence lifestyle, migrating to fish camps in the summer and hunting and gathering in preparation for winter. Yet generations of Native Alaskans have been disconnected from their past, due in part to the birth of the Western education system in Alaska when it became a territory. From plagues to boarding schools, Alaskan Natives have truly suffered (Madsen, 1996).

Again, Alaska is uniquely different, yet technology in some respects, such as social networks, satellite TV, and other media-rich tools, has changed the landscape by offering more possibilities; this new information has connected a once isolated world with the rest of the world. Thus the complexities from this new influence can have a great impact on the efficacy of Native Alaskans' traditional ways of knowing. In the urban areas of Alaska, devices such as cell phones are as common as radios, cafés are patronized based on the availability of wireless services, and features such as online banking are the rule rather than the exception. However, this is not the case in many rural areas of Alaska. Bandwith and cellular phone services are often limited in comparison to Alaska's urban areas. For example, if individuals in Alaska wanted to purchase the Apple iPhone, they would need an address in the Lower Forty-Eight. So-called nationwide cell phone services do not work in most of the villages off the road system, and the new XM and SIRIUS satellite radio services are not available in Alaska. "Officially, neither SIRIUS or XM provide service to Alaska, but both companies acknowledge that they have Alaskan customers. Most are in the southeast portion of the state which is more geographically accessible, while others—such as those in Anchorage—find themselves with a very inconsistent

Figure 6.1. A Holistic Digital Divide Framework

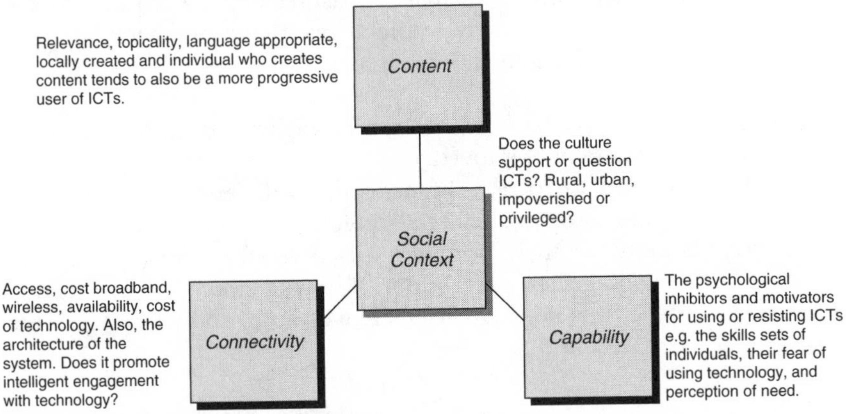

Relevance, topicality, language appropriate, locally created and individual who creates content tends to also be a more progressive user of ICTs.

Content

Does the culture support or question ICTs? Rural, urban, impoverished or privileged?

Social Context

Access, cost broadband, wireless, availability, cost of technology. Also, the architecture of the system. Does it promote intelligent engagement with technology?

Connectivity

Capability

The psychological inhibitors and motivators for using or resisting ICTs e.g. the skills sets of individuals, their fear of using technology, and perception of need.

Source: Based on research by Page (2004).

Note: ICT = information and communications technology.

signal" ("Satellite Radio Is Just over the Horizon," 2006). If service in Anchorage, Alaska, is inconsistent, it is nonexistent in rural areas.

Rural communities struggle for access, equipment, and relevant content when using technology. They seek to join the digital revolution while at the same time seeking to preserve their own identity and culture. Figure 6.1, based on earlier research (Page, 2004) on technology use in a rural area, provides a framework for understanding technology use in rural Alaska. The four areas shown in the figure—content, social context, connectivity, and capability—are reflected in interviews with rural Alaska educators that are described in the next section. First, the responses to specific questions are reported; next the four framework areas are connected to themes that emerged from the interviews.

Interviews with Rural Educators

To gain insight into the context of technology and rural Alaska, interviews were conducted with three rural Alaska educators and technology coordinators from different geographical locations. The purpose was to explore the status of educational technologies, how change and technology are perceived, and what the future holds.

Connectivity Issues. When asked about issues related to connectivity, one district technology coordinator answered as follows:

BOB: Bandwidth, bandwidth, bandwidth!!! There is a vast amount of online material available on the Internet, and the opportunities of groups like the Alaska Distance Learning Partnership [a nonprofit consortium of school districts, education organizations, and Telecom providers that collaborate on ways to provide technology across the vast regions of Alaska] regularly advertise for cost or for free videoconferences. However, bandwidth limitations cause us to pick and choose.

Thus, the diffusion of technology into rural areas will continue to be slow unless connectivity can be improved.

Technology and Culture. The next question centered on the construct of culture and how it is being affected by technology. Culture and Native ways of knowing are important issues in Alaska. Thus, the respondents were asked about their perceptions of how technology was affecting culture: Were the effects negative or positive or both, and why? Again the educators were candid in their responses:

BOB: Culture can be both helped and harmed by technology. The resources available to the technically adept are extreme and varied in their delivery. Technology can record images, movies, and audio from people who will soon disappear and save this information for all time. The ability to understand Native ways of knowing from an elder is invaluable to the individual learning about culture. In this lies the problem. Students are no longer *living* the culture; they are merely *learning* about it.

GARY: As these students grow, they share what they know and value with their parents, and then, eventually, they will be our community leaders. Why, for example, would they pay a consultant thousands of dollars to provide them with information they can find online? In this sense, new technologies should provide an era of self-reliance, independence, and confidence.

Adaptation to Global Change. Global change was another area investigated through the following question: How are individuals in rural areas adapting to global change brought about by the diffusion of information and communication technologies?

GARY: I find that many rural Alaskan adults are wholeheartedly embracing the opportunities presented through technological changes. It allows many the best of both worlds—they get to live in the rural environment of their choosing, yet they have access to most everything, in technological terms, that people living in Anchorage, Seattle, and Paris are able to access. The development of the Web 2.0 tools is a tremendous boon to rural Alaska residents. As long as you have access to the Internet, anyone living anywhere can have access to world-class tools. The most obvious benefit for rural Alaskans is the reduction of the geographical isolation factor. It used to take my students weeks and months of effort to be able to access enough resources to be able to have a decent research paper experience.

New Directions for Adult and Continuing Education • DOI: 10.1002/ace

JOE: The degree of change in rural Alaska over the last five or ten years has been tremendous. In terms of the amount and diversity of information and communication options, I'd say the change has been as big as the "snowmobile revolution" that anthropologists talk about in the 1960s and 1970s. When I first moved to rural Alaska, the villages had one television station (if it was working that month) that came in on the Alascom telephone dish and was rebroadcast just within the village. Diomede, Alaska, for instance, is one of the most remote places in Alaska, and only has a weekly mail flight by helicopter most of the year as a connection to the outside world. Now, adults use voice over IP programs like Skype to talk with whoever they'd like, and buy things, and even watch streaming media. The school has a steerable Webcam that the helicopter service in Nome uses to check conditions before they fly. It's just an amazing amount of change. We Webcast school sports and activities for the Alaska Association of School Activities and some other organizations, and can tell you that there are many, many connected parents and relatives out there tuning in from the villages.

Adaptation to Technology Use. How rural Alaskans are adapting to technology use was another area of interest, and thus participants were asked if they felt information and communication technologies have caused rural adults to become cautious or hesitant about adopting new technologies:

JOE: I would not say that I have run into large numbers of rural residents that are scared of change or are overly cautious. If anything, I think rural residents are eager to have what others have and are not hesitant about adopting whatever private and public entities can offer in the way of technology and communications.

I think that many organizations are struggling with their own acceptance of change . . . certainly there is more reluctance in the institutions that rural adult residents rely on for learning about how to use the new technologies productively than there seems to be in the communities themselves. The school districts, the tribal corporations, the health organizations, and so on are less able to use or train adults on the technologies coming out now. Regional residents have blogs, social networking accounts, and favorites lists on Amazon and are active on their favorite hunting gear forum. We are still worried about teaching them PowerPoint and Word. There will be an increase in Web-based telecommuting soon from rural Alaska. Native artists already are selling carvings and artifacts via eBay and online galleries, and so on. The change is in the air. The problem is whether we have the horsepower to lead in training and equipping students and adults to take advantage of the technology. In the near future, if not already, a young family can have the option to join the cash economy over distance and still keep their traditional folkways and residence in the village. The challenge is going to be for the institutions to remain relevant in a connected world where adults can sign up for accredited or simply engaging course work at the high school and college level . . . without leaving the village. Preparing adult learners to succeed and compete in a participatory Web world does not lend itself well to traditional course progressions. It will become an increasing challenge to get people who have any skill, ability, or interest in technology to want to enroll in these [nontraditional] courses.

GARY: The cost of simply accessing technology can still be relatively prohibitive at the organizational and individual levels. While the number of skilled technology consumers has increased dramatically in rural Alaska, the number of rural Alaskans who are in skilled positions that help support the technological infrastructure has not. All education and training institutions in the state, beginning with the local school district, need to do better work in this regard. I believe there is also the tendency to use new technologies to replace old technologies, but to not utilize them to their full potential. This is largely due to the fact that many rural Alaskan adults are essentially self-taught or learn through informal associations with others.

JOE: As far as actual access challenges, cost is still a factor. We don't have broadband, even though we call it that. We have wireless access, but not the rich infrastructure that connected areas do with fiber backbones. . . . Everything here ultimately has to go on a trip to the equator and bounce off a satellite to an earth station somewhere. That's expensive and drives down the actual amount of connectivity most can afford.

Unless there is a fiber connection via cable laid under the Bering Sea, I don't see much of a change in the overall bandwidth available. I think there is going to be a shortage of available bandwidth as use and expectation increases each year, but the bandwidth does not. We'll have frustrated communities who end up maxing out circuits unless new technologies help out somehow. The rush to Internet2 means nothing to folks out where I live, I'm afraid, as we will not have access unless road or rail connections allow fiber to be laid, or someone comes up with the money to lie commercially nonviable fiber connections to our communities by undersea cable.

Future Projections. A final question asked participants to make future projections by responding to the following question: If you were to look ahead into the near future, what does the shape of technology look like in the next few years for rural Alaskans?

BOB: Currently the rural school district pays around fifteen times the costs of the same bandwidth in an urban Alaskan environment. . . . Add to this the satellite delay, and it is very painful educationally. As all of the schools in the state get around to adding a vast number of computers to the student populations, the students are going to have the tools and the abilities to far outstrip what can be given to them. Computers will continue to get better, and schools will continue to move along at a regular pace, but it will still bottleneck innovation outside of the school district itself. Schools will be able to replicate the social networking aspects of the outside world. We can create wikis and local Facebook, Flickrs, and video transfers, but we will be unable in rural areas to actually take part in the live version. By the time we are able to accomplish what the rest of the world is doing in the now, the world has moved beyond.

GARY: I'd also predict that there will be a surge in small Web and technology businesses being based out of the bush villages, and an increase in adults with technology skills telecommuting from rural locations.

Bridging the Digital Divides. Bridging the digital divides that exist in rural Alaska and the many rural areas of the Lower Forty-Eight will require a commitment to access and infrastructure. Most of all, users and providers will have to traverse the teaching and learning continuum to promote mutual understanding of information and communication technologies as a revolutionary medium that can both preserve and enhance the state of people's lives and livelihood.

Emerging Framework

The effective use of information and computer technologies for education in the rural areas of Alaska necessitates many challenges. The areas of content, connectivity, capability, and cultural context shown in Figure 6.1 are thematic issues around the larger concern of access that emerged from the interviews.

Context. While geographical isolation is becoming less of a barrier, the rate of technology adoption by students in rural areas is slow, cautious, and in some cases hesitant (Janelle and Hodge, 2000). Gary offered this insight into the rural sociocultural context:

> Culture is becoming a side note to technology advances. Culture is becoming something that can be "looked up on Google." With technology bringing the outside world into the rural community, it takes some of the local identity away. This would cause a mixing of the cultures if it wasn't so one-sided. The Internet has taught us that being strange is something to be seen and laughed at on YouTube, and so many of the rural Alaskan kids feel strange enough as it is so they do everything in their power to become less strange.
>
> The Native way of knowing is important not just for answers but also for the process. If the answer was the only thing that was important, then it becomes a result rather than a lesson. Knowing how to fish is more important than the end result of eating the fish. Fishing as a skill is more than subsistence; it is about spending time with those around you.

Capability. Capability refers to the psychological barriers for using technology. The need for guidance, locus of control, self-efficacy, uncertainty about change, fear, and anxiety are examples of this theme. Factors such as resistance or fear of technology are also included. Bill, a rural educator, said, "It seems rural Alaskan entities are in two camps these days: we are scared of some of the technological change, so we are going to limit access dramatically; or, let's find the way to best utilize some of these tools and then share them with people."

Connectivity. Connectivity centers on the broadband connection and the technological infrastructure, that is, the quality and reliability of the connection for access to the Internet. According to Dorr and Besser (2002), connectivity is a major impediment to using information and computer technologies in rural America. This standard has long been the factor used by the federal government to measure access (U.S. Department of Commerce, 1999).

The overall relationship between access and use is much more complex. We must be cognizant that technology can lead to empowerment of adults or further disenfranchisement of the have-nots. Haddon (2000) states, "Information and communication technologies (ICTs) enhance our abilities to fulfill active roles in society, or being without them constitutes a barrier to that end" (p. 389). This issue was the primary impediment according to the rural Alaskan educators interviewed. Bob stated:

> Cost [of connectivity] of everything is an impediment to tech integration because it is so hard to get training for anybody. I am the tech director here, and I receive next to no training in anything year after year. How do teachers get this training? From me? Do you see the problem here? The biggest drawback is that I figure out the way to succeed on my own sometimes merely by force of will. However, this is not the fastest way to achieve things, yet without training, it is the only way I know how. Therefore, it is the only way I can teach. This is echoed throughout rural Alaska. When training is offered, it is expensive sure, but the nontraining costs are very high (airfare, hotel, per diem, etc.). A $1,000 training ends up costing three times that, plus when I am gone, I do not get a sub to do my work.

Connectivity goes beyond just cables and bandwidth. In rural Alaska, it means a link to professional development, education, training, and collegial social networking.

Content. Content is defined as digital information that is created by the individual or is related to the individual's interests (Dorr and Besser, 2002). It is a theme that resounded as the adults interviewed talked about the importance of using computers to create materials related to their interests. The lack of local and relevant content for the rural adult users has an effect on use. It has been called information poverty and is defined as "not knowing what options exist, being an information 'have-not,' that threatens to create a class of electronically colonized info poor techno-peasants" (Cronin, 1995, p. 32).

New Directions for Adult and Continuing Education • DOI: 10.1002/ace

Using the Thematic Issues. Through understanding the factors of content, connectivity, capability, and context, we can better address the complexity of the numerous digital divides in rural areas. Practitioners can be better equipped with this knowledge in order to facilitate digital literacy. Policy administrators and community leaders can better address these issues from a more holistic approach that does not marginalize but builds on the collective Native and rural ways of knowing.

Conclusion

Adult educators face critical issues with effectively using information and communication technologies. Yet few practitioners and researchers have analyzed the operational definitions and specific knowledge base for digital literacies in the lives of adult learners. Rather, digital literacy is often prescribed by technology experts in urban centers, away from the social context of rural communities. Nevertheless, culture, social context, and value systems are interrelated and interconnected to technology. New digital literacies necessitate new challenges for rural educators, such as how to access them, how to integrate them, and how to make them relevant in the rural context through applicable and thoughtful content. Rural and remote information and communication technology initiatives can potentially broaden a gap between the haves and the have-nots and further marginalize, devalue, and deprecate indigenous knowledge. This is the challenge for adult educators: to protect and enhance without diminishing the cultures through a technological hegemony.

References

Albirini, A. "Cultural Perceptions: The Missing Element in the Implementation of ICT in Developing Countries." *International Journal of Education and Development Using Information and Communication Technology,* 2006, 2(1), 49–66.

Cronin, B. "Social Development and the Role of Information." *New Review of Information and Library Research,* 1995, 1, 23–37.

Deniro, S. C. "The Politics of Education Provision in Rural Native Alaska: The Case of Yukon Village." *Race, Ethnicity and Education,* 2004, 71(4), 401–419.

Dorr, A., and Besser, H. "Re-Evaluating the Bridge! An Expanded Framework for Crossing the Digital Divide Through Connectivity, Capability and Content." 2002. Retrieved Feb. 16, 2007, from http://www.newliteracies.gseis.ucla.edu/publications/re-eval_bridge.pdf.

Haddon, L. "Social Exclusion and Information and Communication Technologies: Lessons from Studies of Single Parents and the Young Elderly." *New Media and Society,* 2000, 2(4), 387–408.

Janelle, D. G., and Hodge, D. C. (eds.). *Information, Place and Cyberspace: Issues in Accessibility.* New York: Springer, 2000.

Lenhart, A., and others. "The Ever-Shifting Internet Population: A New Look at Internet Access and the Digital Divide." 2003. Retrieved Apr. 4, 2007, from http://www.pewinternet.org/report_display.asp?r=88

Madsen, E. (ed.). *Yuuyaraq: The Way of the Human Being.* Fairbanks: Alaska Native Knowledge Network, 1996.

Norris, P. (2001). *Digital Divide: Civic Engagement, Information Poverty, and the Internet Worldwide.* London: Cambridge University Press.

Page, G. A. "Exploring the Digital Divide: Poverty and Progress in a Rural County." Unpublished doctoral dissertation, University of Georgia, 2004.

Pittman, J. "Empowering Individuals, Schools, and Communities." In G. Solomon, N. J. Allen, and P. Resta (eds.), *Toward Digital Equity: Bridging the Divide in Education.* Needham Heights, Mass.: Allyn & Bacon, 2003.

Postman, N. *Technopoly: The Surrender of Culture to Technology.* New York: Vintage Books, 1993.

Prakash, M. S., and Esteva, G. *Escaping Education: Living as Learning Within Grassroots Cultures.* New York: Peter Lang, 2005.

"Satellite Radio Is Just over the Horizon." *Anchorage Daily News,* 2006. Retrieved Sept. 14, 2007, from http://www.adn.com/life/story/8153277p-8046030c.html.

Schiller, H. I. *Information Inequality: The Deepening Social Crisis in America.* New York: Routledge, 1996.

Stark, N. "Technology and Grit at the Grassroots: Information Technology, Community Engagement, and Jobs in Distressed Rural Communities." National Center for Small Communities. 2002. Retrieved Feb, 23, 2007, from http://www.smallcommunities.org/ncsc/TechandGrit.htm.

Straub, D., Keil, M., and Brenner, W. "Testing the Technology Acceptance Model Across Cultures: A Three Country Study." *Information and Management,* 1997, *31*(1) 1–11.

Swain, C., and Pearson, T. "Educators and Technology Standards: Influencing the Digital Divide." *Journal of Research on Technology in Education,* 2003, *34*(3), 326–335.

U.S. Department of Commerce. National Telecommunications and Information Agency. "Falling Through the Net: Defining the Digital Divide." 1999. Retrieved Mar. 4, 2007, from http://www.ntia.doc.v/ntiahome/fttn99/.

Williams-Green, J., Holmes, G., and Sherman, T. M. "Culture as a Decision Variable for Designing Computer Software." *Journal of Educational Technology Systems,* 1997, *26*(1), 3–18.

Wilson, J. D., Notar, C. C., and Yunker, B. "Elementary In-Service Teacher's Use of Computers in the Elementary Classroom." *Journal of Instructional Psychology,* 2003, *4*, 256–266.

Wimburg, K. M., and others. "Factors of the Divide." In G. Solomon, N. J. Allen, and P. Resta (eds.), *Toward Digital Equity: Bridging the Divide in Education.* Needham Heights, Mass.: Allyn & Bacon, 2003.

G. ANDREW PAGE *is an assistant professor in the College of Education at the University of Alaska Anchorage.*

MELISSA HILL *is the executive director of Alaska Teacher Placement in Fairbanks, Alaska.*

New Directions for Adult and Continuing Education • DOI: 10.1002/ace

7

Rural workplace learning presents the challenge of reduced resources and increased distance from training providers. The authors looked at five workplace segments and found that each of these has unique needs and barriers to learning.

Workplace Learning in Rural Contexts

Robert F. Reardon, Ann K. Brooks

Hal Jones recently retired after twenty-five years of being a fur trader in Bethel, Alaska. During an interview, he described some of the things that he did to learn this business (personal communication, October 26, 2006). Jones began trapping and selling furs as a teenager in Auburn, Alabama. Around 1965, he met an old man with health problems who trapped and sold furs. Jones befriended him and got him to share his extensive knowledge about selling furs. Soon Jones was buying opossums and raccoons for 50 cents apiece and selling the meat for $3.00 to $5.00 and the skins for about $2.50. In 1965, that was a lot of money for a high school boy.

In 1982, Jones and his wife, Gayle, moved to Bethel, Alaska. There, he began to hunt and trap in the wilderness. At dinner one night, Jones and his friends decided that business would be more lucrative if he became a fur broker. Jones told his friends, "We always complain about the middleman. That is where the money is." Each of the three men put up a few thousand dollars and began buying furs. To start, they offered trappers what they thought were fair prices. In response, the Native Alaskan hunters offered them many more furs than they could afford to buy. They soon discovered that the existing traders had colluded to set prices very low, so Jones's fair price was twice as high as anywhere else.

Jones and his friends had to ship the furs to auction, and this involved a lot of paperwork. Jones went to the U.S. Fish and Wildlife office in Bethel and asked to be shown what paperwork was needed to ship furs to Winnipeg, Ontario. In the process, the men in the office forgot one form, and Jones's furs were seized in Anchorage. Jones managed to get these furs back and eventually bought out his two partners. He decided to improve his business

New Directions for Adult and Continuing Education, no. 117, Spring 2008 © 2008 Wiley Periodicals, Inc.
Published online in Wiley InterScience (www.interscience.wiley.com) • DOI: 10.1002/ace.287

by focusing on buying and selling higher-quality furs. Up to this point, Jones would pay one fixed price to the trapper, no matter what the grade of the pelt. This was called "buying on average." When he sold a load of furs (beaver, for example), he would get paid for as many as thirty-five grades. The range of prices was dramatic between the bottom grades and top grades. In order to learn effective grading, Jones worked without pay at an auction house in Seattle, Washington. During the course of one season at the auction house, he examined as many as 100,000 furs. With two years of experience, he felt much more competent in judging the quality of furs and began to offer his suppliers premium prices for quality furs. By doing so, he was able to increase his profit margin. Meanwhile, his competitors, who continued to buy furs on average, lost the ability to buy premium furs, and their profit margins declined sharply. After a decade of business, the number of fur brokers in western Alaska dropped from twenty-six to one.

This story illustrates one man's process of learning that was specific to the fur business. Of course, Jones also had to learn the other aspects of running a small business, including accounting and paying taxes, and he has increasingly come to rely on the Internet for information. Jones's self-fashioned career illustrates the lifelong learning required of small business-people in the rural United States. It also fits well with the public perception of life in rural America.

Categories of Economic Activities of Rural America

Many people perceive rural America as being an almost completely agricultural, farming, or ranching economy (Greenberg Quinlan Rosner Research, 2002), work that in the public imagination includes such individual entrepreneurs as Hal Jones. In fact, less than 7 percent of rural employment is in agriculture (Porter, 2004); service industries account for over half, and service and manufacturing together account for more than 66 percent of employment in rural areas (McGranahan, 1998). Rural regions take 50 percent of total earned income in service sectors, especially recreation, tourism, and retirement living, and while many view foreign competition as reducing rural manufacturing, recent studies indicate that manufacturing has decreased only in apparel, textiles, and footwear, while remaining strong in construction, mining, rural factories, and high-skill business activity.

Porter (2004) points out that economists have treated rural regions as being different from other areas, leading to different policies and institutions from urban areas. However, although they can be characterized as having lower population density, they cannot be generalized in other ways, and rural regions are influenced by the same basic competitiveness incentives as other regions. Based on a review of the literature, he identifies six categories of economic activity in rural areas: services, farming, mining, manufacturing, government, and nonspecialized. Based on this analysis, we have examined specific industries from each economic segment: tourism and health

New Directions for Adult and Continuing Education • DOI: 10.1002/ace

care; agriculture, forestry, and fishing; mining; education, law enforcement, security, and corrections; and small business.

Tourism. Tourism has become a viable area for economic development in many rural communities (Ohnoutka, 2002) and can include transportation, accommodations, food and beverage services, recreational activities, retail shopping, and entertainment. The needs for worker training range from customer service, public relations, first aid, and food preparation to lodging and housekeeping, water safety, and sanitation and cleaning (Ohnoutka, 2002). In the United States, learning in these areas primarily occurs informally as on-the-job training. Other sources are university extension services (Ohnoutka, 2002); vocational schools and community colleges; and professional associations such as the National Recreation and Parks Association, which sponsors national conferences and workshops and disseminates information regarding trends. The hospitality industry is noted for its large, low-skill workforce (64 percent), lack of formal training structure, high turnover, poor and nonexistent career structures, and absence of a trade union presence (Baum, 2002). In a survey of midsized hotels (150 to 300 rooms) in the United States, a category that would cover many large, rural tourist destinations, Breiter and Woods (1997) conclude that training budgets are low and needs assessments poorly executed. Increasingly, skill shortages in hospitality are viewed as generic rather than technical, demanding communications, people management, and problem-solving training for employees (Baum, 2002). Baum (2002) points to Ireland as an example of successful growth as a tourism destination over the past forty years, which was supported by a sustained investment in integrated hospitality skills development by the National Tourism Development Authority (Fáilte Ireland). The tourism authority provides professional development, primarily through e-learning, tourism colleges, and investment in education at all levels. In the United States, private associations and institutes provide such training to the hospitality industry for a fee in the form of training materials, training libraries, and online courses.

Medicine and Health Care Professions. Health care is changing rapidly because of new procedures, new treatments, and the rapid growth of the older population in the United States. Physicians, nurses, pharmacists, and other health care professionals need continuing education to keep up with their industry's vast and rapid changes. This training is usually mandated by individual state licensing agencies. In addition, the continuing education of these professionals usually has to be approved by the providers' professional organization.

Rural health care providers have always had less access to continuing professional development than providers in urban settings. They are often not close to medical schools or other large medical communities. Providers requiring workplace learning come from all levels of health care and various settings. They include professionally educated practitioners such as nurses, nurse practitioners, physicians, physician assistants, pharmacists, pharmacist technicians, physical therapists, and hospital technicians, as well as aides, housekeepers, and food service employees, who are now trained in such things as universal precautions to prevent the spread of communicable disease. In addition, rural health care workplaces are diverse. They include small doctors' offices, ambulance services, small clinics, and hospitals.

Also driving workplace learning for health care is the fact that the Internet is available to patients and clients. They are able to retrieve information from the Internet and bring additional queries to their local providers. For example, when one of us was recently diagnosed with cancer, he gleaned a lot of information from blogs, Web sites for charitable organizations, and the academic medical literature. This information shaped his questions and decisions regarding his care and treatment. Since health care providers must now converse with a more fluent patient or client, they are forced to stay current on issues.

For nearly two decades, telemedicine has been seen as a solution to providing medical services to remote areas (Stamm and Cummingham, 2005). Telemedicine was initiated as a means to provide specialized medical care to remote areas where specialists were rare. It involved two-way telecommunications of voice, picture, and data between the specialist and health care providers in the remote area. This same technology can provide continuing education for health care providers. More than half of the providers of telemedicine also offer other forms of distance-delivery methods for continuing education, but this form of distance education has the benefit of two-way communication, providing an opportunity for dialogue between instructor and learner (Stamm and Cunningham, 2005). The main barrier to this form of learning is that a limited number of rural sites have telemedicine facilities and trained technicians to facilitate the education.

A much more common tool for continuing education for health care providers is the Internet. A simple search for continuing education with the keywords *medicine, nursing, pharmacy, physical therapy,* and *radiation therapy* revealed dozens of sites for each specialty. Many of the sites advertised that the continuing education being offered was accredited.

A recent study found that rural nurses have particularly felt the lack of learning support and have found technology particularly useful for gaining competence-related skills, but social interaction and support are necessary for overall growth. Rural registered nurses have tended to rely on central information sources such as peers, in-service education, and local newsletters more than on peripheral sources such as the Internet, libraries, and professional journals, with at least one peripheral source of information (Kosteniuk, D'Arcy, Stewart, and Smith, 2006). According to Kosteniuk, D'Arcy, Stewart, and Smith, the Internet is the most common peripheral source in this study. At one hospital, 70 percent of graduate nurses typically quit within the first year. These graduate nurses cited lack of workplace support and job-related stress as principal causes for the attrition. The hospital modified training for graduate nurses from a didactic format to one divided into three areas: venting, case studies, and computer-based training (CBT). Venting allowed the graduate nurses to establish social support within their new environment. The case studies enabled the students to visualize the transfer of relevant skills to complex situations, and the CBT focused on helping them develop specific skills (Squires, 2002).

Agriculture, Forestry, and Fishing. In 2004, the agriculture, forestry, and fishing segments of the economy employed approximately 2.1 million workers, including self-employed and unpaid family members (U.S. Bureau of Labor Statistics, 2007a). Self-employed workers such as farmers and fishers constituted 46 percent of the industry's workforce, and the U.S. Department of Labor projects that work in agriculture, forestry, and fishing will decline, particularly among self-employed workers. These segments are some of the few in the economy for which unpaid family members still constitute an important part of the workforce. Aside from on-site workers, these industries also include support services, mostly to larger farms run on a corporate model (rather than as family enterprises). Twenty-nine percent of the workforce in these three sectors does not have a high school diploma. This proportion is especially high in the agricultural sector, where migrant farmworkers are employed for labor-intensive work.

Traditionally workers in these segments of the economy learned from family and community members. Increasingly for farming, a formal education in business or agriculture is necessary to compete. Professional development usually comes from agricultural journals, county cooperative extension agencies linked to universities, and government research programs.

Over the past three decades, much research has focused on the diffusion of innovations in agriculture (Rogers, 1995). The Cooperative State Research, Education, and Extension Service (CSREES) is an agency within the U.S. Department of Agriculture that helps "agencies provide federal leadership in creating and disseminating knowledge spanning the biological, physical, and social sciences related to agricultural research, economic analysis, statistics, extension, and higher education" (U.S. Department of Agriculture, 2007). Extension services were at one time a common resource for farmers. The CSREES provides funding for agricultural and food research at the nation's land grant institutions and then disseminates the new knowledge through academic publications, extension offices throughout the country, and on its Web site. Although there are over two thousand local extension offices, the CSREES states that it is serving a constituency that is growing and becoming more diverse, with fewer and fewer resources. The organic farming industry is very active in providing information and professional development to farmers. The National Farm Transition Network operates Land Link programs in nineteen states to help match young farmers with those wishing to retire so that land and skills can be passed on to a new generation. Organizations such as the Organic Farming Research

Foundation, the U.S. Department of Agriculture's Alternative Farming Systems Information Center, and the National Sustainable Agriculture Information Service seek to educate organic farmers and build a sustainable agriculture industry.

Another area of workplace learning related to agriculture is the training and education of migrant agricultural workers. Over 7 million unauthorized migrants were employed in March 2005, and they constituted 24 percent of all workers employed in farming occupations (Passel, 2006). Although the U.S. Department of Labor supports some work-related education through block grants administered through the National Farmworkers Jobs Program, United Farmworkers of America provides extensive work-related information to migrant farmworkers regarding workers' rights, organizing, immigration, safety, and voting, among other important topics.

In the logging industry, workers develop their skills through on-the-job training provided by experienced workers and the logging companies. Trade associations such as the American Forest Foundation and the Forest Resources Association provide information, training, and educational materials such as videos, workshops, and curriculum information. State extension services sometimes provide information on sustainable logging practices.

Similar to farming and logging, workers in the fishing industry acquire skills while on the job. One of the few areas of formal training for workers in fishing is mandated safety training. From 1992 through 2002, approximately forty-seven workers died in fishing (National Institute of Occupational Safety and Health, 2006). As a response to the deaths in the fishing industry, the Occupational Safety and Health Administration began a program to provide health and safety training to workers on commercial fishing vessels (Occupational Safety and Health Administration, 2004). The goal of this training was to transfer some of the best practices from other industries (such as manufacturing and mining) to fishing.

Mining. In 2004, approximately 207,000 wage and salary jobs existed in the mining industry, most of these in establishments employing fewer than twenty workers (U.S. Bureau of Labor Statistics, 2007b). Mining is a declining source of employment, in part due to the use of technology in the mining process. Although most workers begin by helping more experienced workers in order to learn skills on the job, formal training is becoming more important due to the increasing use of advanced machinery and mining methods. After passage of the Federal Mine Safety and Health Act of 1977, mines were required to have an approved training program in health and safety related to workers' specific tasks, both for new miners and as yearly refresher training. Interactive training and professional development are available on the U.S. Mine Safety and Health Administration Web site. Many of these materials have been translated into Spanish. High-technology training using machinery and virtual reality simulators has become increasingly common, enabling companies to instantly review miners' skills.

New Directions for Adult and Continuing Education • DOI: 10.1002/ace

As environmental concerns have become more important, those with experience in the mining industry are being trained as environmental professionals, and university graduates in the natural sciences and environmental engineering are being brought into the mining industry and trained. According to many, a training revolution is in the offing due to the demographics of the workforce (transferring knowledge from more experienced to newer workers), the rapid growth of technology, and the importance of the information age (Kowalski-Trakoflier and others, 2004).

Education. Education organizations have several requirements for workplace learning. Teachers are expected to keep abreast of changes in their subject matter, learn and leverage new technology that facilitates student learning, and implement mandated programs such as the No Child Left Behind Act of 2001. In addition to learning needs, continuing education is mandated for most teachers.

Rural schools face many of the same problems as urban schools, yet their resources are often more limited than are their larger urban counterparts. With smaller schools in rural areas, there is a smaller tax base for capital and operating expenses. Until recently, these schools were isolated from new and evolving knowledge by distance.

Computer-based training (CBT) and online training opportunities are possible solutions to the professional development barriers that rural educators face (Jung, Galyon-Keramidas, Collins, and Ludlow, 2006; Summerville and Johnson, 2006). As in other professions, continuing education is available on CD, DVD, and online. Recent changes in online training have included streaming video and interactive teleconferencing with desktop computers. These learning opportunities can range in quality from poor to excellent. In some cases, teachers do not feel that they have the ability to judge the effectiveness of online training and would like to have recommendations regarding quality (Jung, Galyon-Keramidas, Collins, and Ludlow, 2006; Summerville and Johnson, 2006). In the same study, teachers at remote colleges and universities indicated that they would like to continue their education by taking graduate courses.

Many have pointed out that online, CBT, and other technology-driven training do not produce effective teachers. One proposal is that the principles of organizational learning as defined by Senge (1990) and situated learning as conceptualized by Lave and Wenger (1991) must be applied in rural schools to build a cohesive organization (Howley and Howley, 2005). Instead, using local teacher experts in rural professional development may be a more effective means of developing the leadership skills of local teachers (Hickey and Harris, 2005). In summary, the few researchers writing on the professional development of teachers and other school professionals in rural settings seem to be advocating the use of technology for some, but not all, skill development of professional educators.

Law Enforcement, Security, and Corrections. Rural law enforcement agencies have recently faced many changes in the nature of their work. For example, recent federal and state regulations have placed new burdens on rural law enforcement, especially for officers along U.S. borders. Events such as the shootings at Columbine High School in Colorado and the standoff with the Branch Davidians outside Waco, Texas, point to the need for rural law enforcement to plan for contingencies that a few years ago were unimaginable. Illegal narcotics have long been a problem in the States, but their nature, production, and transport change every few years. In addition, new legislation and policies force law enforcement professionals everywhere to modify their procedures. Finally, many correctional institutions are located in rural settings, and unfortunately, the number of Americans in prison is higher than ever before.

Few studies of workplace learning or education of rural law enforcement professionals exist. However, one article did point out correctional officers' need for more continuing education as a result of the increasing number of prisoners, prison crowding, and the growing incidence of psychosocial problems within the prison population (Geiman and Black-Dennis, 2007). As a response, the American Correctional Association recently announced that it was establishing an "Online Corrections Academy" for the training and professional development of prison employees.

Small Business Owners. We began this chapter with an example of a rural entrepreneur learning the ropes of fur trading in Alaska. Like this fur trader, small business operators have to learn the specifics of their trade and the generalities of operating a business. Before they can do this, they have to find sources of reliable information.

Small businesses in rural settings are often faced with logistical barriers. High-speed Internet connections are now available for even the most remote locations. However, the necessary supplies and materials for particular businesses are often not readily available. In order to compete with larger companies, small business operators in rural settings have to learn how to obtain raw materials and ship finished goods in cost-effective ways. This has led to the downfall of many small retail stores in small towns as large-box retailers have moved in (McCune, 1994).

As in the other segments of rural workplaces, online training has become an important tool (Sambrook, 2003; Zager, 2001). It is cited as a means for developing expertise in running a business in general or in business-specific knowledge (Zager, 2001). However, a need for informal and incidental learning still exists and has a strong, positive relationship with job satisfaction (Rowden and Conine, 2005). The development of social networks is an important element of specialized learning.

Manufacturing. As manufacturing has become more technologically advanced, many assume that lower levels of educational attainment among rural populations put rural manufacturers at a competitive risk. However, surprisingly, finding workers with computer, interpersonal and teamwork, problem solving, and other skills, according to one large survey, is no more problematic for rural than for urban manufacturers (Teixeira, 1998). Forty-eight percent of rural manufacturers provided formal training for production workers, and 71 percent had increased their training over the previous three years because of an increased concern with product quality and productivity. Only 37 percent of those increasing training said their reason was low skills among newly hired employees. In fact, rural manufacturers had only slightly more difficulty than urban manufacturers finding workers with specific skills, and for some skills (basic reading, for example), rural manufacturers actually had less difficulty (Teixeira, 1998).

Commonalities of Rural Workplace Learning

Several generalizations exist regarding rural and urban workers, according to a Department of Labor Survey (Gibbs, 1998). First, rural workers tend to be less educated than urban workers. The quality of the K–12 education is similar, but there are more dropouts in rural settings, and the proportion of college graduates is lower than in urban centers. Second, rural firms in most sectors tend to be smaller than their counterparts in urban settings. This may mean they have fewer infrastructures for training. Data from this survey indicated that only 48 percent of rural manufacturers supply formal training to their employees. Third, "high adopters," or firms that tended to employ new technologies to increase productivity or gain other competitive advantages, were more often found in urban settings. "Low adopters," or firms that tended to be manufacturers of commodities that relied on existing technology, were more prevalent in rural settings. In urban settings, only 27 percent of the production firms were low adopters (agriculture, mining, and "routine" production), but these low adopters accounted for 60 percent of the firms in rural settings. When they were located in rural settings, high-adopter firms did more training than low-adopter firms (77 percent versus 40 percent). In addition, 82 percent of the high adopters indicated that they had increased training in the past three years, a much higher number than low-adopter firms.

Sixty-two percent of all the firms in the study reported trouble finding qualified applicants for jobs. The deficiencies noted, in order of the number of times they were mentioned by the firms, were:

- Lack of proper work attitude
- Lack of problem-solving skills
- Lack of noncomputer technical skills (specific job-related skills)
- Lack of computer skills
- Lack of interpersonal skills

High-adopter as opposed to low-adopter firms did not name a lack of proper work attitude as the foremost deficit, leading us to speculate on the

New Directions for Adult and Continuing Education • DOI: 10.1002/ace

relationship between training, especially training in cutting-edge skills, and work attitude.

High-adopter firms found it hard to hire local rural employees with technical skills (for example, engineering and accounting) because many had moved to urban locations. In addition, these same firms found it hard to recruit and relocate employees with technical skills to rural settings. The potential employees resisted, partially because of low educational opportunities for their children and partially because of low opportunities for training and professional development for themselves.

Conclusion

Two main barriers make work-related learning difficult in rural settings. First, rural settings can be remote from centers of power where policies are made; knowledge is generated, stored, and disseminated; and opportunities for professional networking are more abundant. Second, small rural businesses may lack the resources in people and training to acquire or provide learning opportunities to employees. This could occur because rural workplaces are smaller (Gibbs, 1998) and therefore have a smaller capital base for providing training.

The evolving solution to rural workplace learning at first appears to be technology. The cost of distance learning has dropped as technology has improved. High-speed Internet connections, CD and DVD drives, and Web cameras have made streaming video, online training, and interactive workshops possible throughout the country. However, the literature suggests that technology is not a solution to all the training needs in rural settings. Some authors point to the need for more generic skills among both rural and metropolitan workers and point out that these skills go beyond basic and technical skills to focus on communications, people management, and problem solving. In addition, face-to-face involvement appears to be key to employee satisfaction.

References

Baum, T. "Skills and Training for the Hospitality Sector: A Review of the Issues." *Journal of Vocational Education and Training,* 2002, 54(3), 342–264.

Breiter, D., and Woods, R. H. "An Analysis of Training Budgets and Training Needs Assessments in Mid-Sized Hotels in the United States." *Journal of Hospitality and Tourism Research,* 1997, 21(2), 86–97.

Geiman, D., and Black-Dennis, K. "ACA Responds to the Training Needs of the 21st Century Workforce." *Corrections Today,* Feb. 2007, pp. 20–23.

Gibbs, R. M. (ed.). *Rural Education and Training in the New Economy: The Myth of Rural Skills Gap.* Ames: Iowa State University Press, 1998.

Greenberg Quinlan Rosner Research. "Perceptions of Rural America." Battle Creek, Mich.: W. K. Kellogg Foundation, 2002.

Hickey, W., and Harris, S. "Improved Professional Development Through Teacher Leadership," *Rural Educator,* 2005, 26(2), 12–16.

New Directions for Adult and Continuing Education • DOI: 10.1002/ace

Howley, A., and Howley, C. "High-Quality Teaching: Providing for Rural Teachers' Professional Development." *Rural Educator,* 2005, *26*(2), 1–5.

Jung, L. A., Galyon-Keramidas, C., Collins, B., and Ludlow, B. "Distance Education Strategies to Support Practica in Rural Settings." *Rural Special Education Quarterly,* 2006, *25*(2), 18–24.

Kosteniuk, J. G., D'Arcy, C., Stewart, N., and Smith, B. "Central and Peripheral Information Source Use Among Rural and Remote Registered Nurses." *Journal of Advanced Nursing,* 2006, *55*(1), 100–114.

Kowalski-Trakoflier, K. M., and others. "Safety and Health Training for an Evolving Workforce: An Overview from the Mining Industry." In Centers for Disease Control (ed.), *Information Circular/2004.* Atlanta, Ga.: Centers for Disease Control, 2004.

Lave, J., and Wenger, E. *Situated Learning: Legitimate Peripheral Participation.* Cambridge: Cambridge University Press, 2001.

McCune, J. C. "In the Shadow of Wal-Mart." *Management Review,* 1994, *83*(12), 10–17.

McGranahan, D. A. "Local Problems Facing Manufacturers: Results of the ERS Manufacturing Survey." Washington, D.C.: Department of Agriculture, 1998.

National Institute for Occupational Safety and Health. "NIOSH Fatal Occupational Injury Cost Fact Sheet: Agriculture, Forestry, and Fishing." 2006. Retrieved June 27, 2007, from http://www.cdc.gov/niosh/docs/2006-151.

Occupational Safety and Health Administration. "OSHA and Fishing-Vessel Owners Forge Alliance for Job Safety." 2004. Retrieved June 27, 2007, from http://www.osha.gov/pls/oshaweb/owadisp.show_document?p_table=NEWS_RELEASES&p_id=10846.

Ohnoutka, L. "Training Needs of Tourism-Based Businesses." *Journal of Extension,* 2002, *40*(3).

Passel, J. S. "The Size and Characteristics of the Unauthorized Migrant Population in the U.S.: Estimates Based on the March 2005 Current Population Survey." Washington, D.C.: Pew Hispanic Center, 2006.

Porter, M. "Competitiveness in Rural U.S. regions: Learning and Research Agenda." Cambridge, Mass.: Institute for Strategy and Competitiveness, Harvard Business School, 2004.

Rogers, E. M. *Diffusion of Innovations.* (4th ed.) New York: Free Press, 1995.

Rowden, R. W., and Conine Jr., C. T. "The Impact of Workplace Learning on Job Satisfaction in Small U.S. Commercial Banks." *Journal of Workplace Learning,* 2005, *17*(3/4), 215–229.

Sambrook, S. "E-Learning in Small Organisations." *Education and Training,* 2003, *45*(8/9), 506–516.

Senge, P. M. *The Fifth Discipline: The Art and Practice of the Learning Organization.* New York: Doubleday Currency, 1990.

Squires, A. "New Graduate Orientation in the Rural Community Hospital." *Journal of Continuing Education in Nursing,* 2002, *33*(5), 203–209.

Stamm, B. H., and Cunningham, B. J. "The Education Part of Telehealth." *Education for Health,* 2005, *18*(3), 427–431.

Summerville, J., and Johnson, C. S. "Rural Creativity: A Study of District Mandated Online Continuing Professional Development." *Journal of Technology and Teacher Education,* 2006, *14*(2), 347–361.

Teixeira, R. "Rural and Urban Manufacturing Workers: Similar Problems, Similar Challenges: Results of the ERS Rural Manufacturing Survey." In *Agriculture Information Bulletin 736-02.* 1998. Retrieved Apr. 28, 2007, from http://www.ers.usda.gov/Publications/AIB736/aib73602.PDF.

U.S. Bureau of Labor Statistics. "Agriculture, Forestry, and Fishing." 2007a. Retrieved Apr. 27, 2007, from http://www.bls.gov/oco/cg/cgs001.htm.

U.S. Bureau of Labor Statistics. "Mining." 2007b. Retrieved Apr. 27, 2007, from http://www.bls.gov/oco/cg/cgs004.htm.

U.S. Department of Agriculture. *Cooperative State Research, Education and Extension Service (CSREES)*. 2007. Retrieved Apr. 19, 2007, from http://www.csrees.usda.gov/index.html.

Zager, M. "Online Training: A Practical Alternative for Small Business." *Rural Telecommunications*, 2001, *20*(5), 42–45.

ROBERT F. REARDON *is an assistant professor in the education Ph.D. program at Texas State University–San Marcos.*

ANN K. BROOKS *is a professor of adult education at Texas State University–San Marcos.*

New Directions for Adult and Continuing Education • DOI: 10.1002/ace

8

This chapter examines ways that rural character or community can be defined and suggests that future rural adult education research should be framed to include more specific considerations of rural context.

Defining Rural Community(ies): Future Considerations for Informal and Nonformal Adult Education in Rural Communities

Susan J. Bracken

The study and practice of adult education takes place in many forms and contexts, so much so that we sometimes ask, "What isn't adult education?" For the purposes of this chapter, informal and nonformal adult education include just about any endeavor adults undertake to learn and work together outside formal classroom, workplace, or postsecondary educational settings. This chapter examines a basic question about rural informal and nonformal adult education: How do adults who participate in nonformal and informal adult learning activities define rural character or rural community? Building on this discussion, it then makes suggestions for framing future rural adult education research on informal and nonformal adult learning.

Perceptions of Rural Life

Galbraith's past work in rural adult education (1992) characterizes rural communities as having low population densities, limited resource bases, relative isolation, and cultural or ethnic homogeneity. Ritchey (2006) echoes Galbraith by including low population density, but shifts the discussion to include local-based independence, a connection to nature, and shared values or collective responsibility as aspects of rurality. He also discusses

New Directions for Adult and Continuing Education, no. 117, Spring 2008 © 2008 Wiley Periodicals, Inc.
Published online in Wiley InterScience (www.interscience.wiley.com) • DOI: 10.1002/ace.288

change and loss, health care, crime, and technology as important pressing issues. Hobbs (1992) discusses the importance of matching the public's image of rurality to the realities of rural life. He points to the limitations of categories such as metropolitan and nonmetropolitan, assumptions about agriculturally based economies and the lack of acknowledgment of poverty, conflict, brain drain, and transportation as critical elements in understanding what it means to be rural. Like Ritchey, he includes natural resources as an essential element of rural life.

The Kellogg Foundation funded a survey, asking the general public for their images of rural life (Greenberg Quinlan Rosner Research, 2002). The report notes that "perceptions of rural America are based upon dichotomies—rural life represents traditional American values, but is behind the times; rural life is friendly, but intolerant of outsiders and difference" (p. 1). They found that most respondents perceive rural communities to be agriculturally based (the reality is that only 7 to 11 percent of rural communities are agriculture and agriculture-related based) and that they tend to be based on more traditional values. General public perceptions also include an image of rural environments that are safer for families and a less complicated way of life due to distancing from metropolitan areas. These perceptions of rural poverty were based on an image of agriculture, not images that included low-wage service or manufacturing jobs, which is often part of rural life. Survey respondents felt that the core challenges faced by rural communities were lack of money, overdevelopment, crop prices, weather, lack of opportunities, the decline of the family farm, isolation, pollution, education, brain drain, and transportation. They also described rural culture as one epitomized by a strong sense of family, work ethic, commitment to community, strong religious beliefs, self-sufficiency, toughness, a sense of being behind the times, and strong feelings of patriotism. Finally, the survey asked respondents who they believed was responsible for changing and assisting rural communities to sustain themselves and thrive. Nearly half of the respondents felt that the responsibility fell to individuals or communities, with just under 20 percent citing governments as having formal responsibility for sustaining rural communities in the United States.

Over the past several years (Bracken, 2006), I have interviewed, spoken with, and observed fifty-seven community members, half from rural areas in the Northeast and the other half from the Southeast United States. I asked rural residents who were involved in informal or nonformal adult education activities about how they defined "rural," "rural character," and "rural way of life," as well as their opinions about what strengths and challenges they perceived in their activities. Generally perceptions of the public and the literature about rural communities tend to be in agreement with rural residents' identification and naming of the material issues. There is a tie to nature, green space, and population density in rural areas. There are also transitioning or struggling economic and tax bases, changing population demographics, serious community health issues, and difficulty accessing

New Directions for Adult and Continuing Education • DOI: 10.1002/ace

health services. Many rural areas struggle with crime and drugs, poor educational quality, and brain drain. Culturally the emphasis on family relationships and faith was also discussed as critical and unique elements of rural communities. So what were some of the differences or additional characteristics expressed by research participants?

Rural residents talked at length about how they perceived rural culture or rural character, that is, their way of life. They did not frame seemingly competing issues as dichotomies, as did the Kellogg Foundation study. Instead, they perceived issues as complex, multidimensional, or simply a part of a balanced system. Therefore, contradictions or competing interests were assumed to be natural or a normal part of rural life. They talked about the fact that most rural residents value privacy, property rights, and the concept of independence and consequently expect less formal regulation or intervention in their personal and work lives. Rural identity and independence were not characterized just as toughness, self-sufficiency, or creative problem solving due to isolating conditions; they were also described relationally as a right, a preference, a way of being. Social control and collective interests were present, but the idea expressed was that they should be governed more informally, through social peer pressure, collective sense of responsibility, and cooperation rather than through formal rules, regulations, or policies. By implication, informal and nonformal adult education activities often functioned and were understood and judged by community members using this general mind-set. Direct, structured exercises of power were sometimes interpreted as heavy-handed or inappropriate, yet strong and visible informal exercises of power were accepted and supported within rural community action groups.

Furthermore, the perceptions of traditional or conservative family values were somewhat more mixed and diverse than reported public perceptions of rural family values. Many residents were quite progressive in terms of liberal or conservative political views or acceptance of change and diversity as a part of life. Interestingly, tensions or complexities often entered the discussion in terms of the historical narratives. Conflict and cooperation were often dependent on not just the here-and-now, but on an ability to integrate past, present, and future perception of individual actions and communal life. What was particularly interesting was the tendency for participants to view their historical legacies (of family, community, occupation, and others) as positive and essential elements and tools of their personal success in community groups, yet something that they felt was also often misunderstood and unfair when others used the same approach. As an example, one county government employee observed, "I have credibility when I want to introduce a new idea because people here know me, they've known my family background, and they know I understand what will work here . . . but sometimes I wish they wouldn't be so fast to judge me or my ideas by things that happened in the past, things I had nothing to do with or sometimes happened before I was even born." Consistent with Chávez

(2005), participants also discussed their concern about the fact that certain historical narratives appeared to take on a life of their own, overshadowing or silencing other community members' stories as part of a community's collective historical story.

Although social class was not always explicitly mentioned, concepts of economic and social class were at the forefront in discussions of community involvement and rural life. They were often mentioned as a "way of doing things": work ethic, self-reliance, little waste, creativity in problem solving. McGranahan and Wojan (2007) discuss the importance of connecting discussions of rural life and class and of understanding that rural communities may represent a range of class sectors and values. In fact, all of the rural communities I studied had both the classic rural character and aspects of the emerging creative class that McGranahan and Wojan described.

Another reoccurring theme was discussion of the notion of partnership or shared or pooled resources. By necessity, many rural communities do not have the population base for stand-alone services, businesses, resources, community organizations, or programs. Participants stressed that rural families and communities help each other in a time of need and that it is vital to pool and share resources: talents, labor, material resources, emotional and cultural support, and companionship. It is something often taken for granted in metropolitan areas where there is enough population, economic, and municipal size to offer and form stand-alone groups, organizations, or services. Paradoxically, rural community leaders expressed comfort and experience with partnership and pooling resources yet frustration and a feeling of being overwhelmed with the growing complexity and culturally insensitive conditions of forming partnerships outside their local contexts. A point of emphasis in interviews and observations was that rural members of a community often defined their local context with different criteria than did supporting external grant agencies or communities, and this was frequently misunderstood by outsiders as a reluctance to work cooperatively with others. An example of this within the literature is the discussion by Carroll, Higgins, Cohn, and Burchfield (2006) of rural community conflict during times of disaster and the stress that can result when community relationships and ways of getting things done are disrupted by external, extralocal agencies without the flexibility to integrate community ways of being with external approaches.

When community members spoke about adult learning activities, their concerns focused on solving community problems, fellowship, and sustainability. Most participants did not describe their own community action, or learning, as separate from their lives; it was simply a way of being. They expressed a preference for "asking around" to find out who had knowledge or expertise or even a willingness to learn something together, as opposed to more individualistic notions of self-directed learning activities. In the words of one historical society volunteer, "Community means to be civic minded and to always interact with those around you." Most participants said that it was true that a handful of people took the lead on a particular project, but that they believed that most community members acted as both followers and leaders, depending on the situation. Their analysis of how to be successful over the long term in community action or adult learning efforts was remarkably similar to Flora and Flora's description of entrepreneurial communities (1988). They said that it was vital to have an acceptance of controversy, a long-term emphasis on education or learning, enough resources to allow risk taking, private community investment, a willingness to tax or build a tax base that supports community improvement, the ability to see community as a broad concept, the ability to network horizontally as well as vertically with insiders and outsiders, and the ability to be flexible and participate broadly rather than narrowly.

Defining Community(ies)

Many of us automatically think of geography or shared space as a basic starting point in defining concepts of community. By this standard, geographical regions that are low in population density and high in natural resources would be considered rural communities. Within the rural sociology literature, community appears to be predominantly constructed based on two criteria: a shared place (geography) and ongoing interactions (Chávez, 2005). While this is a good beginning point, Chávez cautions that rural community or rural character is also defined by the construction of a dominant narrative, and that understanding rural communities more deeply necessitates exploring nondominant narratives juxtaposed with dominant narratives.

In the adult education literature, communities of practice (Wenger, 1998) are sometimes referred to as sites of adult learning, organized around the principles of shared ongoing activities, structures, and relationships within a group of people. Nyanungo (2006) makes some important points regarding community organizations and groups based on distinctions of whether and how community actions are taking place within a locality or for a locality. This mirrors Ritchey's argument (2006) for the inclusion of responsibility in defining rural communities. In the past, I have relied on Blanco's (1995) application of Royce's work (cited in Kiely, Sandmann, and Bracken, 2006). Blanco defines community as

> a group of individuals that shares a common past, that is a memory; a group that shares a common practice through communication, decision making, and action and thus shares a common present; and a group that shares hopes and plans for a common future infused with values and ideals. To form a community is to develop a public, collective entity—a public mind. This public mind is that part of individual consciousness that is shared, that bridges individual experience, that establishes solidarity among individuals [p. 544].

New Directions for Adult and Continuing Education • DOI: 10.1002/ace

My reason for the use of this definition is that it allows fluid, independent participation and discussions of learning and power (structured and unstructured) without sacrificing the shared public mind or collective consciousness that is a part of any given community. It acknowledges the importance and complexity of history and stories, which my study participants stressed have special significance in rural life. It also allows people to have many minds, not just one mind. As we move in and out of participation in many communities, our own public mind may shift and change or take different forms based on the overlap and separation of those communities and our respective roles. Finally, it allows room for shared understandings of social responsibility to be part of shared community life.

Connecting Rural Community and Adult Education

Not many specific works in adult education have been dedicated to rural adult learning, or rural informal and nonformal adult learning, The exception is the notable historical legacy of agricultural or cooperative extension (McDowell, 2001). Certainly extension has formed a large basis of the program planning and community participation and involvement literature in the field. In addition, grassroots and social movement adult learning contains hints of applicability to rural contexts due to its focus on empowerment, horizontal community participation, or connection to rural issues of natural resources or the environment. Galbraith's edited book (1992) is dedicated to discussions of rural adult education, as are several articles in a 2006 issue of *Pennsylvania Association for Adult Continuing Education Journal of Lifelong Learning* (Coro, 2006; Hiemstra and Poley, 2006; Ritchey, 2006). Next, I found many publications in adult education venues that discuss varying aspects of rural communities and adult learning, though "rural context" is not used as a primary frame or point of analysis for the work. For example, Roberson and Merriam (2005) write about the self-directed learning process of older rural adults, and within that work present a very brief (few sentences) discussion of the fact that learners felt that a rural setting was a positive learning environment. This leads to a question about what we should consider when examining informal and nonformal adult education within rural communities. Given that our potential strategy is to pull from a broad adult education literature on informal and community-based adult education and a scant literature on contemporary rural adult education, I believe there are some basic foundational questions or points to consider:

• *Base future work on rural communities' adult education on contemporary, detailed data and not just on what we assume or perceive to be rural.* Future work in the field needs to more explicitly include information and frameworks based on updated and detailed data about rural communities.

New Directions for Adult and Continuing Education • DOI: 10.1002/ace

Working definitions need to include material or concrete and social or cultural components; either alone is insufficient. Furthermore, studies on rural adult informal and nonformal adult education need to specifically foreground, rather than background, rurality as an essential element of the study framework and analysis. Finally, in addition to literature within adult education, we should draw more extensively from external fields, associations, and information sources.

• *Consider new conceptualizations and frameworks unique to rural adult education.* When I first outlined this chapter, my initial tendency was to go with existing accepted categories within adult education, such as formal and informal adult education, educator and learner, as an expression of rural communities' adult learning. We often draw those lines in the field based on a research participant's membership in a particular volunteer or community action group, organization, or project. When rural population density is low, the cross-membership and roles are exaggerated and not easily viewed as stand-alone. For instance, active community members have very few opportunities for privacy and separation—they grocery-shop, worship, gas up at the filling station, and attend meetings, celebrations, and events often with the same or identical cast of characters; yet as their roles in each of those venues shift, their ability to draw lines or boundaries around their actions or reputations from one venue to the next is diminished. This is influenced by historical and family legacy within rural communities. Therefore, their descriptions of and our understandings of informal adult education efforts do not necessarily fit neatly into preexisting language or frameworks within the field. Arguably, many of the participants in my studies described their community involvement experiences as a way of being rather than as project based, formal, or informal, adult education. Few were willing to draw or accept conceptual boundaries in the same ways that I was imposing those boundaries from the field.

• *Experiment with applying existing frames of analysis that seem especially suited to increase our contextual understanding of rural communities and adult learning.* This final suggestion, like the others, lies in the eyes of the beholder. Based on my interviews and participation in rural communities' adult learning, and also my preferences and knowledge base within the field, I highlight some existing areas of the literature that I believe are a starting point for strengthening the study of adult learning in rural communities. One of the issues that leaped out to me during my own data analysis was the centrality of class consciousness and the relevance of understanding social or economic class and rural adult education. Nesbit's 2005 work on class and adult education points to an absence of class analysis in adult education, and his discussions of Weber and Bourdieu and the reproduction of social class culture are potentially valuable in the study of rural communities and adult learning. Furthermore, Sawchuck (2003) writes of a working-class learning style that is distinctive, solidaristic, and informal and warrants unique attention if cultural outsiders are to understand it. I found that the participants and community leaders in my studies described their participation and learning in ways similar to the way that Nesbit and Sawchuck did. In particular, their pooling of intellectual as well as material resources and preference for patchwork community networking stood out. One of my participants stated, "You are a part of the community when you share a vested interest in the quality of life and when you get involved with sustaining that. . . . You have a responsibility to network your talents because . . . we learn through experiences and problem-solving together, and not through our [nonexistent] formal expertise and credentials." This is one area that is both in agreement and yet different from Roberson and Merriam's work (2005) on self-directed learning and rural adults. Their depiction of self-directed learning was more individualistic than the networked and piecemeal learning and sharing of learning described by my participants and by Nesbit (2005) and Sawchuck (2003). Yet their identification of a catalyst was very consistent with that informal adult learning descriptions I observed. Many of the participants in my studies stated that you needed to be both a catalyst and inspired by others. They stated that they cultivated a pattern of looking for skills and talents others possess that are obvious and not so obvious; they also stressed the need to encourage people to develop their strengths through volunteer involvement.

The next area of existing adult education literature that I believe integrates very well with the study of rural communities and adult learning is contemporary literature on partnerships. All but one of the participants— fifty-six of the fifty-seven—in my study expressed interest, frustration, and extensive experience with internal community partnerships and also with external partners such as universities, schools, nonprofits, and government agencies. There were a few notable hot issues. One was a desire to better develop culturally relevant (meaning rural and ethnic culture) approaches and gain specific formalized training in grant writing and more complex project management, evaluation, and report writing. The integral relationship between the two was emphasized: participants wanted more technical skills only if acquiring them did not sacrifice or decrease the centrality of rural culture to community action. The other consistent hot issue within the partnership realm was a desire to explore the continuum of conflict and harmony that naturally occurs during community or collective action, with a particular focus on the fact that participants know that they are permanently bound together and therefore have a need to preserve relationships in a different way than a community with more inward and outward migration might have.

Finally, within the adult learning theoretical literature, I believe that the scholarship areas of situated cognition and cultural-history activity theory (CHAT) are important and viable areas for exploration. These adult learning theories emphasize sociocultural and historical understandings of communities and learning (Hansman, 2001; Lompscher, 2006; Niewolny and Wilson, 2006; Nyanungo, 2006; Sawchuck, Duarte, and Elhammoumi,

2006). Conceptually they place human situations and human activity at the center of learning and analyze the interrelationships and processes within a given activity system. CHAT also takes into account the concepts of plurality of voices and investigation of contradictions as potential opportunities for learning.

Rural communities have unique, multidimensional cultures and material realities. The existing adult education literature on informal and nonformal learning in rural communities is simultaneously plentiful and full of gaps. Future work in this area needs to be more specific and comprehensive in connecting rural community frameworks to nonformal and informal adult learning frameworks.

References

Blanco, H. "Community and the Four Jewels of Planning." In S. Hendler (ed.), *A Reader in Planning Ethics: Planning Theory, Practice, and Education.* New Brunswick: Rutgers University Press, 1995.

Bracken, S. "Adult Learning and Rural Communities: Defining Rural Community(ies) and Rural Life." Unpublished manuscript, 2006.

Carroll, M. S., Higgins, L., Cohn, P. J., and Burchfield, J. "Community Wildfire Events as a Source of Social Conflict." *Rural Sociology,* 2006, *71*(2), 261–280.

Chávez, S. "Community, Ethnicity, and Class in a Changing Rural California Town." *Rural Sociology,* 2005, *70*(3), 314–335.

Coro, C. "Rural Adult Basic Education in Pennsylvania: Exactly What Do We Know?" *Pennsylvania Association for Adult Continuing Education Journal of Lifelong Learning,* 2006, *15*, 17–31.

Flora, C., and Flora, J. "Characteristics of Entrepreneurial Communities in a Time of Crisis." *Rural Development News,* 1988, *12*(2), 1–4.

Galbraith, M. W. (ed.). *Education in the Rural American Community: A Lifelong Process.* Malabar, Fla.: Krieger, 1992.

Greenberg Quinlan Rosner Research. "Perceptions of Rural America." Battle Creek, Mich.: W. K. Kellogg Foundation, 2002.

Hansman, C. A. "Context-Based Adult Learning." In S. Merriam (ed.), *The New Update on Adult Learning Theory.* New Directions for Adult and Continuing Education, no. 89. San Francisco: Jossey-Bass, 2001.

Hiemstra, R., and Poley, J. "Rural Internet Use Via Broadband Connections: Real Challenges for Lifelong Learning." *Pennsylvania Association for Adult Continuing Education Journal of Lifelong Learning,* 2006, *15*, 85–101.

Hobbs, D. "The Rural Context for Education: Adjusting the Images." In M. W. Galbraith (ed.), *Education in the Rural American Community: A Lifelong Process.* Malabar, Fla.: Krieger, 1992.

Kiely, R., Sandmann, L. R., and Bracken, S. "Overcoming Marginalization and Disengagement in Adult Education: Adult Educators' Contributions to the Scholarship of Engagement." In M. Hagen and E. Goff (eds.), *Proceedings of the 47th Annual Adult Education Research Conference.* 2006. Minneapolis: University of Minnesota.

Lompscher, J. "The Cultural-Historical Activity Theory: Some Aspects of Development." In P. H. Sawchuck, N. Duarte, and M. Elhammoumi (eds.), *Critical Perspectives on Activity: Explorations Across Education, Work, and Everyday Life.* Cambridge: Cambridge University Press, 2006.

McDowell, G. R. *Land-Grant Universities and Extension into the 21st Century: Renegotiating or Abandoning a Social Contract.* Ames: Iowa State University Press, 2001.

McGranahan, D. A., and Wojan, T. R. "The Creative Class: A Key to Rural Growth." *Amber Waves*, 2007, 5(2), 16–21. Retrieved December 27, 2007, from www.ers.usda. gov/amberwaves.

Nesbit, T. (ed.). *Class Concerns: Adult Education and Social Class.* New Directions for Adult and Continuing Education, no. 106. San Francisco: Jossey-Bass, 2005.

Niewolny, K. L., and Wilson, A. L. "(Re)Situating Cognition: Expanding Sociocultural Perspectives in Adult Education." In M. Hagen and E. Goff (eds.), *Proceedings of the 47th Annual Adult Education Research Conference.* 2006. Minneapolis: University of Minnesota.

Nyanungo, H. N. "Participation and Learning in Community Organizations: A Theoretical Framework." In M. Hagen and E. Goff (eds.), *Proceedings of the 47th Annual Adult Education Research Conference.* 2006. Minneapolis: University of Minnesota.

Ritchey, J. A. "Negotiating Change: Adult Education and Rural Life in Pennsylvania." *Pennsylvania Association for Adult Continuing Education Journal of Lifelong Learning,* 2006, 15, 1–16.

Roberson, D. N., and Merriam, S. B. "The Self-Directed Learning Process of Older, Rural Adults." *Adult Education Quarterly,* 2005, 55(4), 269–287.

Sawchuck, P. H. *Adult Learning and Technology in Working-Class Life.* Cambridge: Cambridge University Press, 2003.

Sawchuck, P. H., Duarte, N., and Elhammoumi, M. (eds.). *Critical Perspectives on Activity: Explorations Across Education, Work, and Everyday Life.* Cambridge: Cambridge University Press, 2006.

Wenger, E. *Communities of Practice: Learning, Meaning and Identity.* Cambridge: Cambridge University Press, 1998.

SUSAN J. BRACKEN *is an assistant professor of adult education at North Carolina State University.*

This chapter looks broadly at the preceding chapters, offering some thematic analysis as well as proposing possible areas for additional research.

Rural Adult Education: Future Directions

Jeffrey A. Ritchey

Recently I was part of a conversation that included a colleague currently teaching at a rural, off-campus location recently established by her university. Her teaching at this location was mandated; she neither enjoyed being "out in the boonies" nor felt her instruction would be valued by the "hicks" she assumed lived there. She lamented her classroom full of "rednecks"— an introductory business management course composed primarily of women who, she contended, "only want to get a degree and go home to raise babies." She continued, describing the site's parking lot as full of pickup trucks in a larger community awash in churches, bars, and guns.

This simplistic caricature of rural life stands in stark contrast to the equally stereotypical image often presented of a rural United States bursting with clear running streams, lush green fields, and hard-working women and men who are deeply committed to the protection of their communities and neighbors. As with most other generalizations, the realities lie somewhere in between these two depictions. Nevertheless, these images, simplistic as they may be, remain stubbornly grounded in the collective consciousness— the Beverly Hillbillies and the Waltons; Hooterville and Mayberry—masking the complexity, vibrancy, and possibility of the contemporary rural United States.

As urban centers have grown in size and power, rural areas have increasingly been cast aside as either quaint, somewhat backward relics of our agricultural past or dangerous enclaves of gun-toting, hard-drinking hillbillies. These messages often resonate even among those growing up in

NEW DIRECTIONS FOR ADULT AND CONTINUING EDUCATION, no. 117, Spring 2008 © 2008 Wiley Periodicals, Inc.
Published online in Wiley InterScience (www.interscience.wiley.com) • DOI: 10.1002/ace.289

rural places. As a young man in rural Pennsylvania, I can recall that the definition of success was simple and universally known: you leave. Moving to an urban area, regardless of where or for what purpose, was widely seen as the mark of social success, and my continued conversations (which include a three-year stint as the full-time youth director of a large mainline Christian church) lead me to believe that this has in no way changed. Furthermore, with some demographic exceptions, data from across the United States bear out these anecdotal observations (Artz, 2003). Young people continue to leave rural communities for the educational, cultural, and economic opportunities perceived as being available only in urban and suburban centers.

At one level, this volume has sought to delve beyond the stereotypical to show rural America for what it is: an increasingly diverse social space within which adult and continuing educators continue to play critical roles. This volume is a jumping-off point for what we hope will be more intense and sustained discussions of adult and continuing education in the rural United States. Throughout the volume, some themes have emerged that provide prompts for future directions in research and practice.

A Deeper Understanding of Our Rural Past and Its Role in Our Rural Present

Rural regions of the United States have rich histories that are powerful points of entry to understanding more contemporary social and educational issues. These histories include the sometimes complex relationships that rural places have had with educational and social service agencies, as well as the sociocultural connections communities have with specific industries or occupations.

In short, past experiences, dominant religious and political frames, and reified social roles often define and frame current expectations and reactions. An appreciation of these historical contexts seems imperative for adult educators seeking to develop relationships and extend opportunities to rural residents. In Chapter Two, Zacharakis points out that agencies like the Cooperative Extension Service, with intimate connections to local communities and broad institutional histories in rural places, can play a powerful role in helping to develop grassroots dialogues grounded in a shared past and shaped by a collective future.

In addition, Ziegler and Davis point in Chapter Three to the power of interconnecting community agencies and initiatives and the resultant increases in social, economic, and human capital that proceed from such an effort. This work is grounded in both understanding and challenging reified social and cultural boundaries within communities—boundaries situated in the past but lived out in ever more complex contemporary settings.

New Directions for Adult and Continuing Education • DOI: 10.1002/ace

A Greater Appreciation for the Complexity of Rural Places

To speak of "rural America" as some unified body has become increasingly problematic (if it was ever possible in any meaningful way). The issues facing resort residents in rural Georgia, crabbers on the Chesapeake Bay, or nursing home attendants in New Mexico are diverse and highly localized. While access to reasonable health care, career opportunities, and affordable housing are, at some level, universal in nature, their importance varies from place to place.

What does appear consistent across contexts is the pervasive nature of change in the rural United States. Much of this is a continuation of an economic shift that began as many as fifty years ago, as agriculture, mining, forestry, and other traditional rural industries like steelmaking, textiles, and railroading experienced increased competition and consolidation. Jenkins (2002) notes that Pennsylvania firmly joined the rust belt by 1970 with widespread cuts in the steelmaking, railroading, and mining industries. Furthermore, the amount of Pennsylvania land used for farming began a steady decline in 1950, dropping from 14 million acres to 7.2 million in 2000 (Jenkins, 2002). Although these industries remain a strong part of rural America's collective past, many communities have just as firmly entered the new economy, with "businesses competing in a worldwide marketplace where high-technology and information-based goods and services are increasingly important, and knowledge and information have increased value" (Shields and Vivanco, 2004, p. 5). What is troubling is that many of the jobs associated with this shift—many tied to health, education, and various human services—pay significantly less than the manufacturing jobs they are replacing. Furthermore, as Reardon and Brooks point out in Chapter Seven, many of these rural firms tend to be smaller and may lack the resources necessary to provide learning opportunities to their employees.

Demographically, the rural United States continues to be home to large numbers of older adults. Mott's case studies in Chapter Five make clear the factors underlying the learning endeavors of these older rural residents, from the search for economic self-sufficiency to the creation of more vibrant and challenging retirement periods. At the same time, many areas throughout the United States are experiencing an in-migration of more racially and ethnically diverse groups, many of whom are also younger. In rural areas, demographic shifts such as this, while affecting relatively small numbers of people, may be "more acutely felt" than in areas with larger populations (Jensen, 2006, p. 6). As differences of age, race and language can create divisions in rural places (particularly in relation to social and community services), they can also bring revitalization to populations struggling with the out-migration of young people and a graying citizenry. In Chapter Four, McLaughlin, Rodriguez, and Madden point to the transformative possibilities inherent in these sometimes difficult and complex interactions—a process that often demands the commitment of considerable time and resources on the part of rural adult and continuing education providers.

A Firm Commitment of Time and Resources to Rural Places

When it comes to education in rural places, little can replace the knowledge and sensitivity garnered through a sustained period of time in a specific community or region—indeed, all of the chapters in this volume point to the power of sustained engagement with people in context. Such is the rub at a time when the rapid development of successful (that is, financially self-sufficient or even profitable) educational programs is the norm—particularly when extended to small, rural areas. As noted throughout this volume, the close social networks and relative homogeneity of individual rural communities (as to race, class, educational attainment, and social roles) often mean that lengthy periods of time are necessary to fully understand the lay of the land.

Such knowledge includes the nurture and growth of potential local leaders, the creation of organizational and individual networks for collective action, the identification of appropriate funding streams, and the establishment of safe spaces where people are free to learn and grow in their own communities and to more fully understand the impact of wider, global economic and political actions on their own neighborhoods and families.

A Fuller Understanding of Technology's Specific Role in Rural Places

In Chapter Six, Page and Hill point out that the Internet holds the potential to both connect and divide—to expand opportunities to learn, debate, and create, as well as the potential to open portals for the further development of consumptive culture. Rural people are well aware of these dangers, and if suspicion exists of technology in rural areas, experience tells me that it is with good reason.

Some years ago, I completed a study of a small rural community, looking specifically at the role played by the local church in creating and sustaining communal life (Ritchey, 2002). Satellite television had recently extended myriad viewing options to a community used to only three routinely available channels. The impact was noticeable, particularly in the early evenings when folks would generally take walks or young people could be seen in the summer months riding bikes or hanging out in the church parking lot. As satellite dishes proliferated, people began to disappear in similar numbers—many now busy with *Seinfeld* reruns or *Wheel of Fortune*.

Yet the advent of DSL and other technologies also holds great promise for rural residents—as a means for accessing information and developing networks and reaching distant political leaders, and as a way for rural residents to learn computational and research skills that are increasingly seen as basic. E-mail proficiency, the use of various software packages, and some skill at using search engines for information gathering are viewed as essential to many new economy positions that are forming the foundation of the rural workplace. Once again, however, Page and Hill astutely point out that viewing such educational possibilities as grounded solely in connectivity is simplistic and shortsighted.

A More Enthusiastic and Creative Research Agenda in Rural Places

All of this new understanding leads to the need for a more enthusiastic, aggressive, and creative research agenda for rural adult education. Although survey data and statistical analysis continue to be available in abundance through the U.S. Department of Agriculture and a growing cadre of nonprofit rural assistance agencies, the highly contextual nature of rural community building and adult educational programming means a more sustained and intimate understanding of localized ways of learning and interacting. In Chapter Eight of this volume, Bracken touches on several of these, including cultural-historical activity theory and situated cognition. I would add communities of practice, social learning theory (Lave and Wenger, 1991; Wenger, 1998), and social capital theory (Putnam, 2000; Fields, 2003). All of these theoretical frames speak to the complex and often unarticulated aspects of learning, and both see the educative process as intimately and inextricably tied to the social networks of a given context.

"Communities of practice are groups of people who share a concern or a passion for something they do and learn how to do it better as they interact regularly" (Wenger, n.d., p. 1). Learning in such groupings is often not the intent but results as an incidental part of the groups' interactions. Wenger makes clear that practice involves "doing in a historical and social context that gives structure and meaning to what we do" (1998, p. 47). As such, it is emergent, involving the whole person and not limited to "traditional dichotomies that divide acting from knowing, manual from mental, concrete from abstract" (p. 47).

While the term has been used in many ways, *social capital theory* is largely concerned with articulating the social networks and norms of reciprocity within a specific community. This process provides a potentially powerful means by which educators can better understand how knowledge is created and shared within specific places.

As might be expected, both theoretical frames demand sustained and significant investments of time and attention on the part of educators and practitioners already pressed for resources. Yet as we have seen, an increasingly complex rural countryside demands such intensive and imaginative approaches if our work is to remain vibrant and effective.

New Directions for Adult and Continuing Education • DOI: 10.1002/ace

References

Artz, G. "Rural Area Brain Drain: Is It a Reality?" *Choices: The Magazine of Food, Farm and Resource Issues,* 4th quarter 2003, pp. 11–15.

Fields, J. *Social Capital: Key Ideas.* New York: Routledge, 2003.

Jenkins, P. "The Postindustrial Age: 1950–2000." In R. M. Miller and W. Pencak (eds.), *Pennsylvania: The History of the Commonwealth.* University Park: Pennsylvania State University Press, 2002.

Jensen, L. "New Immigration Settlements in Rural America: Problems, Prospects, and Policies." Durham: Carsey Institute, University of New Hampshire, 2006.

Lave, J., and Wenger, E. *Situated Learning: Legitimate Peripheral Participation.* Cambridge: Cambridge University Press, 1991.

Putnam, R. *Bowling Alone: The Collapse and Revival of American Community.* New York: Simon & Shuster, 2000.

Ritchey, J. A. *The Role of Religion in Shaping the Rural Context: A Study of a Small, Rural Community in Pennsylvania.* Lewiston, N.Y.: Edwin Mellen Press, 2002.

Shields, M., and Vivanco, C. "Rural Pennsylvania and the New Economy: Identifying the Causes of Growth and Identifying New Opportunities." Harrisburg: Center for Rural Pennsylvania, May 2004.

Wenger, E. "Communities of Practice: A Brief Introduction." N.d. Retrieved Jan. 3, 2007, from http://www.ewenger.com/theory/communities_of_practice_intro.htm.

Wenger E. *Communities of Practice: Learning, Meaning and Identity.* Cambridge: Cambridge University Press, 1998.

JEFFREY A. RITCHEY is an assistant professor of adult and community education at Indiana University of Pennsylvania.

INDEX

The chapters in this volume outline in practical terms the research-based applications of possible selves that have relevance for adult educators. ISBN 978-04701-8329-8

ACE113 Teaching Strategies in the Online Environment
Simone C.O. Conceição
One of the challenges for adult educators who teach online is identifying teaching strategies that fit the needs of learners, content, and the environment. This volume describes a variety of teaching strategies, research on their use in the online environment, examples of how they have been used in online courses, a consideration of their effectiveness and limitations, and implications for the practice of adult and continuing education. ISBN 978-07879-9674-1

ACE112 Challenging Homophobia and Heterosexism: Lesbian, Gay, Bisexual, and Queer Issues in Organizational Settings
Robert J. Hill
This volume is designed for professionals interested in building safe and inclusive work and learning environments for adults related to sexual orientation, gender identity, and gender expression (lesbian, gay, bisexual, transgender, and queer people, LGBTQ). Readers will gain knowledge, skills, tools, and resources to identify sexual minority needs; cultivate LGBTQ networks and ally groups in work settings; dismantle the lavender ceiling that prevents sexual minority mobility in organizations; interrogate heterosexual privilege and fight homophobia; design and implement nonharassment and antidiscrimination policies; achieve domestic partner benefits; and build best practices into organizational strategies. It explores sexual identity development in the workplace through the lens of transformational learning theory and opens new ways to think about career development. In addition, this volume offers unique insights into lesbian issues in organizations, including the double bind of sexual orientation and gender discrimination. Some of the chapter authors look specifically at educational settings, such as the continuing professional development of K–12 teachers and the dynamics of dealing with sexual orientation in higher education, while others focus on business workplaces. The volume concludes with an analysis of public policies and organizational practices that are important to LGBTQ lives, with a focus on how organizational policy can make space for the emergence of difference related to sexual orientation and gender identity. ISBN 0-7879-9495-2

ACE111 Authenticity in Teaching
Patricia Cranton
Authenticity is one of those concepts, like soul, spirit, or imagination, that is easier to define in terms of what it is not than what it is. We can fairly easily say that someone who lies to students or who pretends to know things he or she does not know or who deliberately dons a teaching persona is not authentic. But do the opposite behaviors guarantee authentic teaching? Not necessarily. Becoming an authentic teacher appears to be a developmental process that relies on experience, maturity, self-exploration, and reflection. It is the purpose of this volume to explore a variety of ways of thinking about authenticity in teaching, from the perspective of scholars who dedicate themselves to understanding adult education theory and

research and from that of practitioners who see themselves as working toward authentic practice.

The contributors address five overlapping and interrelated dimensions of authenticity: self-awareness and self-exploration; awareness of others (especially students); relationships with students; awareness of cultural, social, and educational contexts and their influence on practice; and critical self-reflection on teaching.
ISBN 0-7879-9403-0

ACE110 **The Neuroscience of Adult Learning**
Sandra Johnson and Kathleen Taylor
Recent research developments have added much to our understanding of brain function. Though some neurobiologists have explored implications for learning, few have focused on learning in adulthood. This issue of New Directions for Adult and Continuing Education, *The Neuroscience of Adult Learning*, examines links between this emerging research and adult educators' practice. Now that it is possible to trace the pathways of the brain involved in various learning tasks, we can also explore which learning environments are likely to be most effective. Volume contributors include neurobiologists, educators, and clinical psychologists who have illuminated connections between how the brain functions and how to enhance learning. Among the topics explored here are basic brain architecture and "executive" functions of the brain, how learning can "repair" the effects of psychological trauma on the brain, effects of stress and emotions on learning, the centrality of experience to learning and construction of knowledge, the mentor-learner relationship, and intersections between best practices in adult learning and current neurobiological discoveries. Although the immediate goal of this volume is to expand the discourse on teaching and learning practices, our overarching goal is to encourage adult learners toward more complex ways of knowing.
ISBN 0-7879-8704-2

ACE109 **Teaching for Change: Fostering Transformative Learning in the Classroom**
Edward W. Taylor
Fostering transformative learning is about teaching for change. It is not an approach to be taken lightly, arbitrarily, or without much thought. Many would argue that it requires intentional action, a willingness to take personal risk, a genuine concern for the learner's betterment, and the wherewithal to draw on a variety of methods and techniques that help create a classroom environment that encourages and supports personal growth. What makes the work of transformative learning even more difficult is the lack of clear signposts or guidelines that teachers can follow when they try to teach for change. There is now a need to return to the classroom and look through the lens of those who have been engaged in the practice of fostering transformative learning. This volume's authors are seasoned practitioners and scholars who have grappled with the fundamental issues associated with teaching for change (emotion, expressive ways of knowing, power, cultural difference, context, teacher authenticity, spirituality) in a formal classroom setting; introduced innovations that enhance the practice of fostering transformative learning; and asked ethical questions that need to be explored and reflected upon when practicing transformative learning in the classroom.
ISBN 0-7879-8584-8

NEW DIRECTIONS FOR ADULT & CONTINUING EDUCATION
Order Form
SUBSCRIPTIONS AND SINGLE ISSUES

DISCOUNTED BACK ISSUES:

Use this form to receive **20% off** all back issues of New Directions for Adult &
Continuing Education. All single issues priced at **$23.20** (normally $29.00)

TITLE	ISSUE NO.	ISBN

Call 888-378-2537 or see mailing instructions below. When calling, mention the
promotional code, JB7ND, to receive your discount.

SUBSCRIPTIONS: *(1 year, 4 issues)*

☐ New Order   ☐ Renewal

U.S.	☐ Individual: $80	☐ Institutional: $195
Canada/Mexico	☐ Individual: $80	☐ Institutional: $235
All Others	☐ Individual: $104	☐ Institutional: $269

Call 888-378-2537 or see mailing and pricing instructions below. Online
subscriptions are available at www.interscience.wiley.com.

Copy or detach page and send to:
John Wiley & Sons, Journals Dept, 5th Floor
989 Market Street, San Francisco, CA 94103-1741
Order Form can also be faxed to: 888-481-2665

Issue/Subscription Amount: $ _____	**SHIPPING CHARGES:**
Shipping Amount: $ _____	SURFACE Domestic Canadian
(for single issues only—subscription prices include shipping)	First Item $5.00 $6.00
Total Amount: $ _____	Each Add'l Item $3.00 $1.50

(No sales tax for U.S. subscriptions. Canadian residents, add GST for subscription orders. Individual rate subscriptions
must be paid by personal check or credit card. Individual rate subscriptions may not be resold as library copies.)

☐ Payment enclosed (U.S. check or money order only. All payments must be in U.S. dollars.)

☐ VISA ☐ MC ☐ Amex # _____ Exp. Date _____

Card Holder Name _____ Card Issue # _____

Signature_____ Day Phone _____

☐ Bill Me (U.S. institutional orders only. Purchase order required.)

Purchase order # _____
Federal Tax ID13559302   GST 89102 8052

Name_____

Address _____

Phone _____ E-mail _____

JB7ND